The Entrepreneur's Incentive

As pocket watches go, it was rather big and clumsy, but then it was never designed to be a pocket watch. Instead it served a much higher purpose as a ship's chronometer. While the timepiece was beautiful in its handcrafted execution, replete with fine engraving and detail, it was fundamentally a marvel of mechanical accuracy. So accurate, in fact, that it was probably the most valuable timepiece ever created. You see, this was the winner of the cash prize authorized by the British parliament in 1743, the solution to the complex longitude problem and the pride of its entrepreneurial creator, John Harrison.

None would argue that the current state of the automotive industry is not in dire need of a fix, whether the topic for reform is sales, safety, economy, energy or efficiency.

My contention is that great solutions to any problems of the day are most often the result of the tireless efforts of a driven entrepreneur in pursuit of a worthy reward and not the government or any of its "fix-it " programs. It just isn't the government's most shining moment to attempt to innovate, let alone create.

Historically, however, the entrepreneur has risen to the task when the proper reward was associated with a clear quest. In 1919, a $25,000 prize for the first non-stop aircraft flight between New York and Paris, with the associated Atlantic crossing, was offered by New York hotel owner Raymond Orteig. After several years and many unsuccessful attempts by others, Charles Lindbergh took the dare and on May 20, 1927, made the successful record flight in 33½ hours to claim the reward.

While most of us remember the Lindbergh event, few know that more than two centuries before the New York-to-Paris challenge was announced, the British Parliament, in 1714, offered a prize of 20,000 pounds ($12 million today) for a solution in the form of a device or invention for determining longitude that "shall have been Tried and found Practicable and useful at Sea." As you can imagine, this announcement captured the imagination and attention of inventors, astronomers and mathematicians alike.

The solution, and therefore the prize, fell to a simple village carpenter from Barrow, England, by the name of John Harrison. It wasn't easy. In spite of his brilliance, his efforts were spurned, thwarted and ignored by scientists of the day and bureaucrats of all levels. Only the driving tenacity of the entrepreneur held on and outlasted the varmints to eventually claim the prize.

Horse racing promoters have known this secret for centuries: If you want the wonderful horses to run in your race, you must have the fantastic winning potential of a fat purse.

There must be a clear consensus as to what constitutes the quantitative parameters of a goal and an appropriate monetary incentive. Judge it fairly, quickly and impartially – then stand back and let the entrepreneurs congregate and create.

Drive in Peace,

Gerry Durnell

Gerry Durnell
Editor & Publisher

New Hanover County Public Library
201 Chestnut Street
Wilmington, North Carolina 28401

1

Automobile Quarterly

The Connoisseur's Publication of Motoring
– *Today, Yesterday, and Tomorrow* –

GERRY DURNELL
Editor & Publisher

KAYE BOWLES-DURNELL
Associate Publisher

JOHN C. DURNELL
Chief Operations Officer, Technical Editor

TRACY POWELL
Managing Editor

LARRY CRANE
West Coast Editor

RALPH KRAMER
Technical Editor

JOHN EVANS
Chief Financial Officer

DAN BULLEIT
Art Director

ROD HOTTLE
Administrative Assistant

ROBIN JEFFERS
Customer Service

RONNY SEALS
Restoration Technician

L. SCOTT BAILEY
Founding Editor and Publisher

Contributing Photographers
CARL BRAUN, LARRY CRANE
CLIVE FRIEND
WINSTON GOODFELLOW
CRAIG WATSON

Contributing Writers
JEROEN BOOIJ, BROOKS T. BRIERLEY
DAVID BURGESS-WISE
LARRY CRANE
LEIGH DORRINGTON
MARIO LAGUNA, KARL LUDVIGSEN
L. SPENCER RIGGS

www.autoquarterly.com

ISBN 1-59613-063-6   (978-1-59613-063-0)

Printed in Korea

Contents

VOLUME 49, NUMBER 3 • THIRD QUARTER 2009

Cover: Mosaic by Steve Maloney.

The Pegaso Adventure
A Bull by the Horns

Unlike many of my fellow compatriots, I have never taken a bull by the horns, but when I first felt the wood-rimmed Nardi steering wheel of a Pegaso in my hands, I instantly remembered what Z-102 designer Wifredo Pelayo Ricart asked Carrozzeria Touring boss and friend Carlo Felice Bianchi Anderloni. He wanted to give a Spanish touch to the Milan-produced Superleggera body to dress the new Pegaso. Anderloni's answer was the reminiscent bull's nostrils in the distinctive Pegaso's engine hood. As in the noble, yet fierce, animal, the holes in the aluminum sheets work as vital air intakes.

BY MARIO LAGUNA

"La aventura Pegaso," by master painter Alfredo De la María, depicts ENASA 0102.152.0115 at the 1952 Monaco Grand-Prix. Opposite: Serra spider 0102.153.0166 starred at Don Siegel's Spanish Affair. Inset above: Count Caralt races Touring 0102.150.0150 at Montjuich in 1954.

Packed with the most advanced technology of its time, in the body and mechanically, the brand-new Pegaso amazed auto specialists, car journalists and the public alike when it was introduced at the 1951 Paris Motor Show.

Made in a truck and coach factory in Barcelona, an aerodynamic, fully operational concept car known as Pegaso Cúpula was for sale at New York's World Motor Sports Show in February 1953. It was outrageously expensive at $29,000, but Wifredo Ricart ironically justified the involvement of Spain's Franco government in the making of his dream brainchild: "We are a poor country and therefore we must make jewels for the rich."

The first 2.5-liter alloy quad cam Z-102 engine, 75mm bore/70mm stroke, met with the new 1952 Grand Prix regulations. A 5-speed transaxle gearbox, rear inboard drum brakes, De Dion axle and sodium-cooled exhaust valves were sophisticated additions. Advanced specifications featured by the 1951 Empresa Nacional de Autocamiones, Sociedad Anónima (ENASA) berlinetta were too many to list but included a V8 light-alloy casting engine; dry-sump lubrication; forged aluminum pistons; torsion bar suspension; telescopic steering column; and a strong, welded, pressed-steel, short-chassis body.

Keeping the same V8 block, capacity was further increased with bore modifications to 2.8-liter 80mm bore, and then to 3.2-liter 85mm bore.

ENGINE Z-102

Type	102 B/2.5	102 B/2.8	102 B/3.2
Number of cylinders	V8-90°	V8-90°	V8–90°
Cubic capacity	2.472 cc	2.814 cc	3.178 cc
Bore and stroke	75 x 70 mm	80 x 70 mm	85 x 70 mm
Compression ratio	7.7:1 8:1	7.7:1 8:1	7.7:1 8:1
Fuel octane number	80 NO	80 NO	80 NO
Power factory tested *	nc	152 hp at 5,000 rpm	208 hp at 6,000 rpm

*Average power for engines with four double-choke Weber carburetors and 90 NO fuel, less for other models with one or two carburetors and 80 NO fuel. A 282hp-at-6,000rpm power record for a 3.2 compressed engine using M20 fuel mix was factory registered on May 6, 1955.

DIMENSIONS AND WEIGHT
(in meters and kilograms)

	Standard	Sport
Length	4.085	"
Width	1.58	"
Height	1.29	"
Wheelbase	2.34	"
Ground clearance (adjustable)	1.27 to 1.60	"
Track front	1.32	"
Track rear	1.29	"
Dry weight	1.060	990

The elegant Serra spider 0103.150.0104 had to live with a 1.4-liter Seat engine. Insert: ENASA catalog introduced the Pegaso prototype 0102.150.0101 in 1951.

Above: The Ricart family in 1925. From left, José Ricart, Wifredo Ricart, Wifredo Jr., age 3. Below: ENASA berlinettas were on display at the 1951 Salon de Paris and available for customer road tests.

WIFREDO RICART

Born into an old, wealthy family, Wifredo Ricart (1897-1974), was highly educated. His father José Ricart Giralt (1847-1930) was the director of the Nautical School in Barcelona. At the age of 10, young Ricart was one of the two subscribers in Barcelona to international aviation magazines. As a new engineer, he joined with Pérez de Olaguer to build their own brand, Ricart y Pérez. He then designed the Ricart-España in a new association with Felipe Batlló. In 1936, Ricart moved to Italy and worked as consultant for Alfa Romeo boss Ugo Gobbato. At Alfa Romeo, he designed advanced racing cars such as Type 162 and Type 512, with central-mounted flat-12 engine.

Soon after, Ricart had to flee Italy when allies progressed from Sicily to the industrial North region, where Alfa Romeo factories were located. Previous experience at Alfa Romeo as head of both the Special Projects Section and the Design Section was valuable; it enabled Ricart to cope with the complexity of organizing the huge ENASA factory and the research and homologation center Centro de Estudios Técnicos de Automoción (CETA) in postwar, ruined Spain. Juan Antonio Suanzes, president of the Instituto Nacional de Industria (INI), later promoted to Industry minister, charged Ricart with the organization and direction of CETA and ENASA, both created in 1946.

Government-supported ENASA bought the ancient Hispano-Suiza factories in Barcelona for the strategic, first-priority task of building trucks and coaches, an essential contribution to Spain's transportation needs in its post-Civil War relaunching. Railroad construction was difficult in a country which is the second most mountainous in Europe.

Ricart persuaded INI to fund the production of an advanced car as a better and faster way for specialized, technical apprenticeship. Young technicians would learn in different fields during the process of building the car; they would get practical experience and in the future would lead the Spanish car industry. That was a pragmatic approach, which, in theory, was also cheaper than training teachers and building technical schools. Nonetheless, it is not totally true that the project Z-102 was accomplished only by apprentices. Many experienced former workers of Hispano-Suiza were recruited by ENASA, and Wifredo Ricart also

Berlinette luxe PEGASO Z-102/2,5

Left: ENASA prototype 0102.150.0101 was finished in the first quarter of 1951, ready for its first road test. Right: Touring spider Le Mans 0102.153.0145 at Villa d'Este in 2004. Below: Strong pressed-and-welded steel ENASA chassis was shared by all Pegaso production.

brought to CETA qualified technicians, mathematicians, designers and engineers who worked with him at Alfa Romeo, in particular young Ettore Pagani, who played an important part in Z-102 development.

PEGASO IDENTIFICATION

The chassis and engine serial numbers give us the essential information of a Pegaso sports car. Cast in exposed spots on the frame, the pillar below the battery and the engine, a series of 4-3-4 digits are a primary source of information. The first four digits, 0102, are common to all Z-102 production. CETA (see above) is the Spanish spelling for Z, and 102 was the project number for the first 2.5-liter Pegaso engine, hence Z-102.

Code 150 was chosen for LHD cars, while code 153 represents RHD cars. The last four digits are the correlative production number of the car. For example, serial number 0102.150.0101 points us to the first Z-

102 Pegaso, which was LHD.

For engines, capacity differences can be read in the three central digits; 011s are 2.5-liter, 017s are 2.8-liter and 019s are 3.2-liter engines. Number 016 denotes a compressed engine. Engine number 0102.019.0162 points to a 3.2-liter engine that matches chassis 162.

THE BODY QUEST

The prototype and preproduction cars were dressed in-house by ENASA designers recruited in Italy. Early Z-102 cars were known as ENASA Berlinetta or Barcelona Berlinetta because of the factory location. The styling followed the Batista Farina's Cisitalia aerodynamic-integrated concept. One of these cars, #0113, took class honors at 1994 Pebble Beach Concours d'Elegance. Today, the lost prototype may look crude in period car magazines, but when ENASA public relations man, aristocrat Fernando de Sentmenat, took it out of the factory for an early press photo in the first quarter of 1951, it was unanimously acclaimed as one of the purest breed GTs of its time.

The ENASA models were 100 percent factory built from scratch, from whole engines and body sheets to the last nut and bolt. Auxiliary industry, nonexistent in postwar Spain, forced CETA and ENASA to design, build and test every single car's component, which was the reason why Z-102s were so expensive.

In 1952, Wifredo Ricart traveled to interview Pierre Saoutchik in Paris and Carlo Felice Bianchi Anderloni (1916-2003) in Milan. Ricart knew the Pegaso needed not only styling improvements to sell in bigger numbers, but also lighter construction to ease the brakes' effort, one of the car's weaknesses. Only 12 ENASA berlinettas were built, including renumbered cars on the same chassis – a nightmare for marque specialists when tracing their history. The reasons for such a dubious practice were different. A works racing car, for example, could be refreshed, renumbered

Pegaso prototypes display at Barcelona factory in 1952. Clockwise from top: ENASA berlinetta, Saoutchik coupe, Touring berlinetta and Saoutchik cabriolet.

and sold as new to a customer.

The era of externally designed Pegaso bodies started with two open cars, introduced at the 1952 Salon de Paris. Instantly, the fresh Touring spider known as Tibidabo, #0118, appeared as a much more modern car than the retro-looking, baroque Saoutchik cabriolet, #0116. Although Saoutchik redesigned a smooth Series 2 with integrated fenders, when bankruptcy occurred by 1954, a mere 18 units had left the Parisian shop.

Touring gave to Pegaso the most beautiful car in the GT world. Arguably, the Pegaso Touring berlinetta has one of the best-looking side views of the entire '50s

GT production. Without unnecessary ornamentation, its beauty oozes from a well-balanced, harmonic sculpture.

When Bianchi Anderloni signed a contract with Ricart for the production of a short series of Superleggera bodies, Enzo Ferrari left Touring for Pinin Farina. Ferrari feared the Pegasos would look too much like his cars if they were designed by the same coachbuilder. In 1953, a Pegaso by Touring cost 500,000 Spanish pesetas, with 10 percent of that being import taxes for the body alone.

The cars in the last series of Touring-bodied Pegasos were identified with the new Z-103 code and were

One of the Saoutchik cabriolet series in Barcelona in 1954.

It is confirmed that a few works and experimental cars were scrapped in house. Also, in the last days of the Z-102 and Z-103 project, when it was buried by the above-mentioned Suanzes, several bare chassis, engines and parts were scrapped. A few unfinished cars escaped a black fate and lived with Jaguar, Alfa Romeo or even Seat engines, but the idea of a lost, unknown Pegaso is only a myth.

With a very narrow margin for error, the production figures, listed by body types, must be as follows:

PEGASO PRODUCTION	
ENASA	Number of units
berlinetta	12
Cúpula #0102.150.0121	1
Bitorpedo #0102.153.0110	1
Racing works cars	4
Bare chassis for motor shows	1
Total	**19**
TOURING	
berlinetta	24
Spider Tibidabo #0102.150.0118	1
Thrill #0102.150.0133	1
Racing works cars	2
Spider Le Mans	3
3-volume hard top	1
Z-103 Panoramic windshield	8
Total	**40**
SAOUTCHIK	
Coupe	14
Cabriolet	4
Total	**18**
SERRA	
Spider	7
Total	**7**
TOTAL PEGASO PRODUCTION	**84**

supposed to be equipped with a detuned version of the well-known Z-102 engine. The new V8 Z-104 engine arrived too late, witnessing Pegaso's swan song at its last international public appearance at the 1956 Paris Motor Show.

The last Pegasos with Z-103 bodies had lost the peculiar engine lid and the distinctive front-end cross. They are recognizable because of their panoramic windshield.

In order to avoid strong import taxes and therefore to build less expensive cars, Wifredo Ricart turned to domestic coachbuilder Pedro Serra, who did a fine job hand-building a short number of Z-103 spiders.

The 1955 Serra #0103.150.0102 is the only one of the entire Pegaso production to legitimately be considered a brand-new car, as it was never sold. It remained for 54 years within the factory walls, with the exception of a couple of press road tests. In addition, it is the only Pegaso bearing a simpler Z-104 engine.

COUNTING PEGASOS

Despite ENASA never making public its production data and no proper Pegaso registry, it is more than certain that fewer than 100 Pegasos left the factories in La Sagrera (Barcelona) and, for the last units, in Barajas (Madrid).

RACING VERSIONS

In three consecutive years, Pegaso entered races for the World Championship, without success. Wifredo Ricart always said Pegasos were not purposed-built racing cars. Nevertheless, in 1953, ENASA made a record car, known as the Bitorpedo, inspired by Taruffi's Bisiluro but featuring a central front engine and pilot sitting on the right axle. Innovative solutions included a pilot-operated aerodynamic brake, similar to the one used by the 1955 Le Mans Mercedes-Benz 300SLR.

In 1952, the Monaco Grand Prix was open to sports cars instead of the traditional single-seated cars. For the first time in Spain's postwar history, a proud national team entered a World Championship race. The ENASA berlinettas raised some eyebrows at the tortuous urban circuit during practice. Fading brakes arose as a major problem and forced Ricart to withdraw his team before the race.

With brand-new racing spiders designed by Touring, the Pegaso team traveled to La Sarthe for the 1953 Le Mans 24-hour race. Two spiders, #0145 and #0155, were works entered for Juan Jover/Prince von Metternich and Joaquín Palacio/Julio Reh.

When practicing, Juan Jover had a serious accident under the Dunlop arch and nearly lost a leg in the crash.

Again, Ricart decided not to race the spare team.

For the 1954 Carrera Panamericana, Spain couldn't officially enter a Ferrari and a Porsche challenger because of the delicate diplomatic relationship with Mexico.

Pegaso accepted an offer from General Rafael Leonidas Trujillo to race a car under the Dominican Republic flag. Trujillo was the first owner of the 1953 New York's Pegaso Cúpula, also known as El Dominicano.

Joaquín Palacio was fast and had a chance racing a third Touring spider, #0142. The powerful supercharged Pegaso proved trouble-free on roads above altitudes of 2,000 meters. Unhappily, Palacio totally wrecked the car when in third position, chasing the leading Ferraris.

The racing program failure didn't stop works driver Celso Fernández from bravely writing the only Z-102's victorious chapter, breaking speed records at Jabbeke in September 1953 for the flying kilometer and the flying mile at, respectively, 243.079 km/h and 241.602 km/h.

Pegasos were regular contenders in local rallies in the hands of private drivers, and they claimed discrete victories in national trophies at Montjuich and Barajas.

Antonio Creus raced Touring spider 0102.153.0155 at Spa-Francorchamps in 1956.

THE DRIVING EXPERIENCE

To honor the widespread international fame and the level of technical sophistication of Pegaso, the famous Pebble Beach Concours d'Elegance had a special class for the Spanish car in 1994. Thirteen Pegasos answered the call to gather at the lawns of the golf course, the largest number yet to be admired in a single American venue.

The 50th anniversary of the marque was remembered by the Centro de Cultura Contemporánea de Barcelona (CCCB) with a big exhibition in 2001. Visitors admired 11 Pegasos under one roof, some of them Pebble Beach veterans.

However, Pegasos are not confined in museums or exhibits. They regularly are seen competing at historical road races such as Mille Miglia in Europe or Colorado Grand in America. Such exotic cars are eligible for the world's most prestigious events.

When writing his book *La aventura Pegaso*, the author had the privilege of sharing the cockpit and, on occasion, the wheel of a few pristine representatives of the Z-102 generation.

Recently, he experienced the ability of the 1955 Salon de Paris Pegaso Touring berlinetta to cope with real traffic conditions on open roads. For an automobile designed almost 60 years ago, the throttle response is vigorous, with the power transmitting instantly to the tarmac. The ideal 50/50 weight distribution helps to balance the car through bends and hairpins, while the anatomically correct belted seats offer good lateral support for the driver. The clutch is

Le Mans Touring spiders at La Sagrera, Spain, in 1953.

heavy to floor and the unusual gear-lever arrangement, with mirror shift pattern, needs some practice, but a Pegaso offers a thrilling experience to the fortunate custodians of the approximate 40 survivors in working condition.

Becoming a foreign moneymaker was a failed mission for the Pegaso sports car. To show the world Spain's advanced technology, on the other hand, the Pegaso gave ENASA good publicity for truck and bus exports in significantly increased numbers.

As Great Britain's *The Autocar* pointed out, extensive design and engineering resources made Spain's Pegaso a car with which to be reckoned. Though fans around the world were aware of the Pegaso's advanced technology and beautiful design, its lack of development forced a sudden ending without heirs. AQ

Pegaso Z-102

EMPRESA NACIONAL
DE AUTOCAMIONES, S.A.

SPAIN

LAGASCA, 88
TELEPHONE 25 93 95
MADRID

LA SAGRERA, 179
TELEPHONE 25 14 24
BARCELONA

CABLE ADDRESS
«AUTOCAMIONES»

Seen today, the lightweight 1955 Salon de Paris Touring berlinetta.

Everything

But The Motor
The Dunhill Story

*H*enry Ford once famously said that the purchase of the car was only the beginning of the transaction, but in fact a young Englishman had discovered that fundamental truth long before the days of the Tin Lizzie. Alfred Dunhill, who had inherited his father's company shortly before his 21st birthday in 1893, was perhaps the first to realize that the new-fangled horseless carriage as delivered – headlights, horns and the like were not part of the specification – was a blank canvas on which the pioneer automobilists of the day could, by adding their choice of accessories, indulge their creativity and pride of ownership.

BY DAVID BURGESS-WISE
PHOTOGRAPHY BY CLIVE FRIEND

The Dunhill business on the busy Euston Road in North-West London had been founded 100 years earlier by a Dunhill ancestor who was "concerned with outfitting for horse traffic." Under Alfred's father Henry, it had supplied the sacking and tarpaulins vital to the horse-drawn commercial traffic that crowded London's streets, as well as harnesses and "horse leathers, saddlery and accessories for carriages." Young Alfred had joined the firm as an apprentice harness maker in Queen Victoria's Golden Jubilee year of 1887; he also traveled with a pony and cart selling carriage blinds. The streets of Britain still echoed with the clatter of hooves and the rumble of carts, but a few hundred miles away across the English Channel, the first successful motor cars were hissing and puttering their way on to the highway.

We don't know precisely when young Alfred Dunhill discovered the motor vehicle, but three years after he took over the company, the antique law requiring a man to walk in front of every motorized vehicle was repealed and the speed limit was raised from four to 12 miles per hour.

The new act came into force on November 14, 1896, and Harry Lawson, the pint-sized entrepreneur who was attempting to secure a monopoly of the infant British motor industry, celebrated the new freedom of the roads by organizing the first London-to-Brighton rally on that red-letter "Emancipation Day." It's easy to imagine that young Alfred Dunhill was one of the thousands of eager spectators who lined the streets to see the procession of motor vehicles pass by on their 60-mile journey to the Sussex coast, and he quickly grasped the potential of the new mode of transport.

The following year, he launched into the manufacture of motor accessories, for which he coined the name "Motorities," offering such practical items as "real cape leather gloves, with double palms for driving, 3s 6d a pair, will wear out six pairs of ordinary gloves and gauntlets to reach up to the elbow for use when starting or attending to the machinery." Recalled Alfred Dunhill, who had grasped the new opportunity for capitalizing on the expertise in leather working that his father had

Your Motor-cycle —and Dunhills

Some Dunhill Motorities.

Goggles. Lamps
Oilskins. Leggings.
Motor Clothing.
Wind Screens.
Generators. Grids.
Sidecars.
Horns and Whistles
Speed Indicators.
Voltmeters.
Accumulators.
Batteries.
Lodge Plugs, etc.
Switches.
Valises.
Tool Kits.
Repair Kits.
Soldering Outfits.
Motor Oils.
Belts, etc.
Vulcanisers.
Etc., Etc.

IT is all very well to picture that whirl through the countryside as one long spell of unbroken pleasure, but it is more practical to reflect on the possibilities of mishap and to anticipate the troubles that may arise. It is still more practical to arm yourself with all those "Motorities" which add to the joy and enable you to deal promptly and effectively with "troubles." It is not good to find yourself in difficulty just as the shades of night are falling and you at a spot "miles from anywhere." Be a "road-wise" motorist and equip yourself fully and efficiently at Dunhills.

Drop us a card as to what you require, and we will send you particulars and quotations

Dunhill's LIMITED,
LONDON—359-361, Euston Road, N.W.1.
Telephones – 3405 and 3406 North.
GLASGOW—72, St. Vincent Street.
Telephone – 7649 Central.

established: "I quickly discovered that there were scores of things wanted for the new mode of travel – leather coats, knee aprons, caps with special flaps to afford extra protection, goggles, veils, foot muffs, special funnels, tools, clocks, and even first aid sets. By these means I attracted practically the whole motoring public to the out-of-the-way premises near King's Cross which, though central for the original trade, were inconvenient for the new class of customer."

And it was a class of customer that was growing with amazing speed; in 1897, there were an esti-

mated 650 cars in use in Britain. By the time registration numbers were introduced in 1904, there were 8,500 private cars on the road. The number doubled a year later and trebled in 1906.

Dunhill's bold venture must have paid off quickly, for he soon was seen at the tiller of a solid-tired, Coventry-built, twin-cylinder Daimler, Britain's first true production car, which, with a price tag in the region of £300 ($1,350), cost as much as a family house.

As early as the spring of 1900, Alfred Dunhill boasted, "My new illustrated catalogue contains 101 good things … especially designed for your requirements." He established a satellite business a short walk away from his premises, on Euston Road. At Motor Mart, private owners could buy, sell and exchange their cars and motorcycles; a magazine was published there under the same name. Motor Mart's manager was a go-ahead young fellow named Eardley Billing, who in later years would become famous as the joint proprietor, with his wife, of the Blue Bird Café which catered to the pioneer aviators at the

Dunhill offered a bewildering array of horns, including the multinote Testaphone (page 14) and the convoluted Scroll Horn (right).

Brooklands Aerodrome and Race Circuit.

Motor Mart only charged commission and storage, a policy that was well liked by its clients. Typical was the testimonial received in 1903 from titled motorist Lord Willoughby de Eresby, who wrote from his country seat near Stamford in Lincolnshire. "I write to acknowledge the receipt of cheque for my motor which you have sold for me. I am fully satisfied with the sale, and consider that the amount you have charged for commission is very moderate, including as it does, two months' garage."

Another automobilist, R.A. Tutt, praised Motor Mart's unbiased advice. "I have much pleasure in giving you a testimonial in regard to the 6½-hp Darracq car you sold me. I have just finished a tour round Norfolk and Suffolk, and the number of miles we did from Monday to Saturday was 600, which is a good test for any car, and as I took your advice when buying this car, I have proved it a great success. When I am buying another car I shall certainly come to you."

The Autocar was impressed by the new venture's bustling way of doing business, commenting in October 1901: "A good plan has been adopted by Mr. A. Dunhill at the Motor Mart, Euston Road, as, for the convenience of callers, a notice board has been

fitted up in the passage where all the latest entries to the Motor Mart can be seen. This enables anyone in a hurry to keep in touch with the newest additions to the showroom with the minimum expenditure of time."

Summer or winter, there were motoring coats to suit every season in Dunhill's stock, in linen, leather or a whole menagerie of exotic animal skins.

Soon after, however, the ambitious Eardley Billing resigned his position as manager and set up as the Central Motor Company, just off Tottenham Court Road, hiring out motor bicycles.

The Motor Mart lasted a few more years, but quietly faded away as the Dunhill Motorities business burgeoned. Keeping Motorities and Motor Mart discretely separate had enabled Alfred to remain true to his proud motto "Everything but the Motor."

In 1903, Dunhill opened West End showrooms just off Regent's Street in Conduit Street – Rolls-Royce

motor coats designed for popular makes of cars, such as the Lanchester ("made in drencher-proof tweed"), the Napier ("stylish Russian foal skin"), the Decauville ("gives complete protection from dust"), the Panhard ("very smartly made in fawn"), and the Beaufort ("smart natural seal … particularly adapted for motoring as it can be washed with soap and water").

Weather protection was almost nonexistent on most early 1900s automobiles, thus the catalogue additions of "Umbrella Coats," the "Motorist's Hand Protector" (a fur-lined waterproof leather bag that covered the steering wheel and the driver's hands and wrists), and "Dunhill's Patent Freer Apron, the most perfect form of Motor Apron yet introduced … designed to fit closely to the legs, thereby giving ample space for steering pillar, ignition manipulation and pedal control."

Dunhill also offered bizarre, fur-lined, leather face masks, designed to protect motorists from wind, dust and flying insects, and furry foot muffs ("lined lambskin 6s 6d, puma £2 10s").

Photographs of motorists wearing these warm but cumbersome garments made them look like hairy Michelin men, so Alfred Dunhill, realizing the importance of sex appeal in selling clothing, used a drawing of a glamorous short-skirted cutie in cap, goggles, leather jacket and calf-hugging knee-boots to promote his "chic motoring attire and equipment."

Nevertheless, the proprieties of the day had to be observed, which is why the company maintained two separate showrooms, at Nos. 2 and 5 Conduit Street. The curious code of Edwardian morals – which turned a blind eye to the clandestine affairs that were

Hats aplenty (above). Among the myriad mascots on offer was this combined radial aeroengine and MotoMeter for the sporting aviator (left).

de rigueur at weekend house parties – considered it improper for ladies and gentlemen to buy articles of clothing in the same shop.

In 1904, Dunhill's headquarters moved in a more fashionable direction along the Euston Road to an impressive corner site that incorporated showrooms, workshops and offices. It was presumably where those strict society conventions dictated that the chauffeurs and footmen of the nobility and gentry came to try on their Dunhill liveries at a suitably discreet distance from their similarly occupied employers.

That year, too, Dunhill's motoring clothes collected a gold medal at the International Exhibition of Dress, Clothing and Textile Industries at London's Crystal Palace.

Motor clothing was only part of the picture, for already Dunhill's 130-page catalogue included an impressive 1,334 motoring accessories. Since October 1903, these had included perhaps the most bizarre item Dunhill ever offered, the result of an unfortunate encounter between Alfred Dunhill and the notorious police speed trap along the Fairmile at Cobham, where the Portsmouth Road that ran southwest out of London emerged into the country from suburbia. This was the domain of the infamous Sergeant Jarrett, who gained rapid promotion through the numbers of

and Austro-Daimler would be neighbors – where he sold such gems as the "Patent Collapsible Bexhill Goggles," which "folded into a small case for the waistcoat pocket," and a whole menagerie of fur and leather clothing made from such exotic skins as opossum, squirrel, mink, chinchilla, seal, Russian foal, kid, lambskin, leopard and puma. There were also ladies'

motorists he arrested for exceeding the speed limit.

Reports do not confirm whether it was Jarrett himself who was manning the speed trap when Alfred Dunhill drove cautiously down the Fairmile, but the semifarcical proceedings have all the hallmarks of that much-reviled policeman.

Dunhill complained, "The evidence produced was a police sergeant, who stated he had timed me over a measured 440 yards, that he had started his stopwatch as I passed a post 434 yards away from him, and stopped it as I passed a post six yards beyond him, and that I had traveled the distance at the rate of 22 miles per hour. There was no corroborative evidence of any sort offered by the police as to the pace I was going. The sergeant admitted in cross-examination that I at once stated he had made a mistake, and that I offered to take him over the distance without altering a lever on the car to prove my statement. This he refused to do, saying it was not his duty.

"I then went over the distance myself, going at exactly the same speed as previously, and stopped in front of the sergeant, who said he wished I had gone six yards further, as then he could have taken the time, but as far as he could make out, I had taken about twice as long as on the previous occasion."

Asked to interview a witness to obtain a statement in Dunhill's favor, the police sergeant refused, on the grounds that his tea was getting cold.

Incensed, Alfred Dunhill, who already offered goggles "in infinite variety," created binocular goggles known as Bobby Finders, which were intended to allow motorists to detect hidden police traps. They were guaranteed to "spot a policeman at half a mile even if disguised as a respectable man." The basic model "fitted with four lenses" cost two guineas ($9.45), and a deluxe version with six lenses was three guineas ($14.20). Alongside the Bobby Finders, Dunhill offered a remarkable chronometer known as the Spedograph (Snelgrove's Patent), accurate to one-tenth of a second, which also gave an instant read-out of the speed in miles per hour

The *Contour Road Book* (right) was an essential part of the touring equipment for the pioneer automobilist, detailing the hills en route.

over a measured distance. Other Motorities intended to keep the long arm of the law at bay were "speed indicators of every make for motor cars" and "tell-tales for back lamps," for a common cause of prosecution in the early days of motoring was that the obligatory oil rear lamp had blown out.

Headlights were an important item in the Dunhill catalogue. The Dunhill "Duplex" dual lens acetylene headlights, as supplied to moneyed scorchers such as press baron Alfred Harmsworth, who fitted them to his 60hp Mercedes now preserved in Britain's National

Motor Museum, were claimed to produce a fearsome 2,500 candle power, a light "so intense that a newspaper can be read with ease at a distance of 150 yards. No wonder Dunhill boasted that "to ride behind this lamp is a thrilling experience."

And to cope with the result of the bumps and scrapes that afflicted so many pioneer motorists in those predriving test days, Dunhill operated a "lamp hospital" where "lamps in the last stage of collapse are speedily renovated and those with only minor faults are carefully attended to." The service was later extended to include damaged radiators and wings ("no case is considered too bad for treatment").

A combined altitude recorder and barometer was another 1903 offering, along with a combined toolbox and pneumatic foot cushion and spring-loaded waterproof leggings. Whatever the motorist required, Dunhill's catalogue was ready to fill the gap, offering a panoply of such "interesting and useful devices" as the Dreadnought handmade headlight, the Adnair jack, the Umbrella Dust Shield, folding ladders "for loading baggage on to the roofs of closed cars," eight-day dashboard clocks, "triple and single exhaust whistles," vacuum flasks, luncheon baskets, tea baskets and Dunhill's Scroll Horn, "possessed of a very powerful and deep note." All kinds of luggage, from trunks for the luggage grid to circular valises to fit inside the spare tire, were available. There was even the "Neptune" portable bath, "suitable for the Continent."

For those with leather lungs, there was Dunhill's four-note horn. Commented the helpful catalog, "With this instrument one can play all the tuneful coaching calls so familiar in the last decade."

For those of lesser lung power, there was the deluxe version, "with flexible brass tubing and foot-plunger bellows for supplying air pressure."

And if Dunhill didn't supply the motor, it did offer a range of modest wooden garages, "made in sections and easily assembled by unskilled labor."

When the new Brooklands track opened in the summer of 1907, the ingenious Mr. Dunhill was at hand to offer his services. With no precedents to guide them, committee members of the Brooklands Automobile Racing Club followed horse racing practice and decreed that as an aid to identification, drivers should wear racing silks, with their colors entered in an impressive ledger. Alfred Dunhill advertised

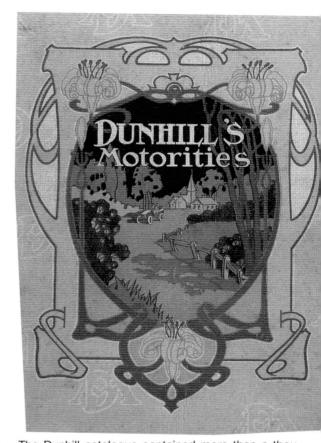

The Dunhill catalogue contained more than a thousand "Motorities," including the magnificent "Duplex" dual-lens acetylene headlights (left).

that he could make "racing colors for Members of the Brooklands Club at short notice in silk, linen and wool." But *The Autocar* complained that "colors which were quite prominent when the cars were at rest became indistinct when they were moving at high speed, and the numbers painted on the cars were altogether invisible." Those racing silks lasted little more than a season.

As time rolled on and cars became better equipped, so Dunhill adapted its offerings to suit. The flight of fellow accessory manufacturer Louis Blériot across the English Channel in the summer of 1909 inspired Alfred Dunhill to cater to the needs of the owners of the new-

types of goggles, some with tinted glass in cobalt blue, gray, yellow or deep green. But weather protection was improving; most cars now had adequate windshields, and only racers and sportsmen needed goggles.

Motor accessories of the immediate pre-World War I period were aimed more at the growing number of motor tourists and included the Dunhill Speedometer, Clock and Auto Route, a combined instrument that was a sort of mechanical ancestor of satellite navigation, in which a strip map unrolled in time with the progress of the car, an invaluable aid to navigation provided the motorist didn't deviate from the ordained route.

By then, Alfred Dunhill had withdrawn from the day-to-day running of the company to devote himself to new projects and was to be seen at the wheel of a square-rigged, British-built, 1912 Model T Ford Runabout, a car remarkably at odds with the Motorities philosophy of accessorizing the vehicle to

Apart from clocks and interior lights for luxury limousines, Dunhill also offered motoring pipes, including one designed by Malcolm Campbell.

fangled flying machines with a range of "Avorities." (The magazine *Aeroplane* thought the word "cacophonous … as repulsive as the actual things are attractive and comforting to the wearers.") The new slogan was "Everything but the Aeroplane," and the range of aviation accessories included compasses and barographs, flying suits, face masks, leather-lined stockings and a fetching choice of safety helmets, including a positively medieval device with a steel collar and crown, covered in leather and padded with felt.

The Motorities era reached its peak around 1910, when the catalogue offered a remarkable 1,457 different accessories, including more than 30 different

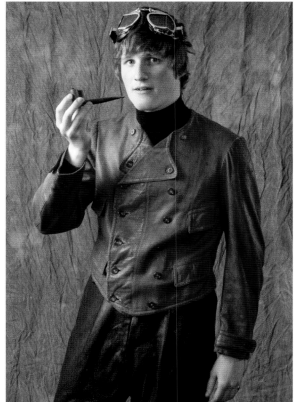

the hilt, for it appeared to be in standard Trafford Park trim, apart from the addition of a Stepney spare rim in case of punctures. A later mount used during the war years was a vee-twin Harley-Davidson "Silent Gray Fellow" motorcycle with a coachbuilt sidecar, a product line the Dunhill company had been offering since 1905. For a short while Dunhill also marketed motorcycles, acting as agents for the sporty Regal-Precision marque.

And in 1912, the company overturned its long-time boast of "everything but the motor" by taking on the agency of the French-built Tweenie cyclecar, a basic little machine with a twin-cylinder engine and crude sliding-pillar independent front suspension. Its friction drive gave a remarkable seven forward speeds and offered "rapid acceleration, top-gear hillclimbing and handiness in traffic akin to the attributes of a high-powered motorcycle." Records show that around 110 Tweenies were sold between 1912-14. Happily, the last surviving Tweenie was acquired for the Dunhill Museum in the late 1990s and now can be seen wearing a range of accessories from the company's collection, including a dashboard clock, altitude recorder, horn, headlights, map-reading light and combined oil and fuel can.

Wartime activities created a huge increase in demand for Dunhill's smoking products, and a new catalog was entitled simply "Things the Soldiers are asking for!" Among those soldiers was Alfred's son, Alfred Henry, an officer in the Queen's Royal Regiment, who returned home after the Armistice with a Military Cross for taking 400 German prisoners.

The 1920s saw a radical change in Dunhill's market. The demand for Motorities dwindled, for cars were now sold ready-equipped with headlights and horns, and the growing popularity of sedans meant that there was no longer a viable market for specialized motoring clothing. Elaborate picnic sets and footwarmers – in fact, "everything for the tour" – took over.

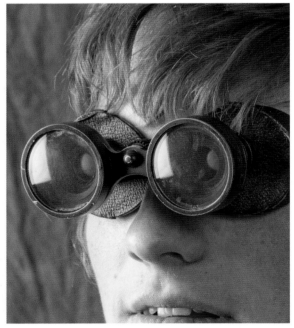

Picnic sets, maps and gauntlets were other items in the Motorities range, while the "Bobby Finder" binocular goggles were for detecting speed traps.

Also growing in popularity were watches and lighters for the Bright Young Things, whose style icon, the Prince of Wales, was a dedicated Dunhill customer with his own special entrance to the company's new London shop in Duke Street in the heart of West End club land. Here, a ramrod-straight, uniformed commissionaire named Jeffrey ushered customers into the imperious presence of the morning-suited, monocled manager Major Malcolm Somerset, late of the King's Household Cavalry, whose impressive client list included such society luminaries as Winston Churchill, Noel Coward, Somerset Maugham, P.G. Wodehouse and Ivor Novello. Film stars such as Douglas Fairbanks and Rudolph Valentino looked in when they were in town. W.O. Bentley was a Dunhill customer, and speed king Malcolm Campbell was not only a customer of but also a designer for Dunhill, inventing a briar pipe that was claimed to be "eminently dry and cool-smoking." King George VI was among its devotees.

Dunhill branch shops had opened before the war in Manchester and Glasgow, and in 1921, a New York branch opened on Fifth Avenue, moving to the Rockefeller Center in 1933. A Paris branch opened on the swanky Rue de la Paix in 1924.

Dunhill had become the "ultimate lifestyle brand," and Alfred Dunhill's bushy-bearded brother Bertie believed in living the ultimate lifestyle, directing the company's international empire from his villas in the Italian Alps and at Monte Carlo, where he dallied with a succession of exotic mistresses. One of them, the lovely Frederika Agnes Stodolowksy, was the wife of a Dunhill employee who had conveniently been given a one-way ticket to Australia. Alfred, too, fell under the spell of the high life and ran off one day with a fisherman's daughter in his Rolls-Royce. He retired in 1929 and was succeeded by his son Alfred Henry. By then, Motorities had faded from the catalogue. Perhaps the last item appeared in 1930, a two-dimensional Mickey Mouse mascot designed to be affixed to the radiator honeycomb. But there were still echoes of the company's motoring past. Racing drivers Earl Howe and Sir Henry

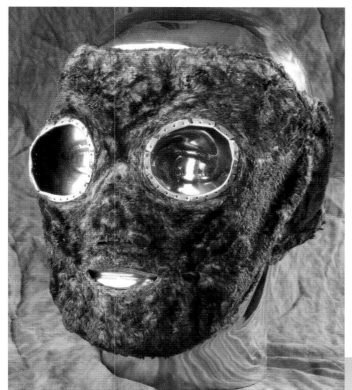

from Lake Coniston, where he had crashed in his Bluebird jet boat.

The 1990s saw Dunhill reconnect with its motoring past. The company became a major sponsor of the Goodwood Festival of Speed and joined with one of motoring's most iconic marques, Aston Martin, to create the Alfred Dunhill Aston Martin DB7 – hailed as "the first result of a long-term program of cooperation between the design teams of Aston Martin Lagonda and Alfred Dunhill." Finished in an exclusive platinum body color with charcoal, Connolly hide upholstery embossed with the Alfred Dunhill logo, the Dunhill DB7 was lavishly equipped. The statement that "this will be the first ever DB series Aston Martin to be fitted with an Alfred Dunhill humidor, which will keep cigars in pristine condition for an indefinite period of time" was unlikely to be contested. Other items unique to the

model included a silver cigar cutter, a purpose-made cigar lighter and a set of Alfred Dunhill AD 2000 pens housed in the lid of the central armrest.

Customer response to the model was so enthusiastic, the Dunhill DB7 was available in all 29 countries where Aston Martins were sold, but ultimately just 78 Dunhill DB7s out of a proposed edition of 150 were built in 1998-99, making this unique model a greater "ultimate indulgence" than the special identity plate indicated.

Custom luggage sets for luxury marques Bentley and Maybach followed, as did a special-edition Egli-Vincent motorcycle. The purchase of a leather factory in North London saw the introduction of a range of Motorities clothing inspired by original items in the company museum and complemented by the introduction of drivers' watches and fashion accessories with a motoring theme.

Dunhill may have moved on from the days of "everything but the car," but to the lover of luxury there remains, as the eponymous Alfred used to say, "always something new at Dunhill." AQ

This fearsome face mask was intended to protect the complexion in the days before windshields became standard, while the Distance Meter (right) helped calculate the length of a journey.

"Tim" Birkin were regular customers in the 1930s, and suave film star Adolphe Menjou purchased a gold lighter in the shape of a Rolls-Royce radiator. There were even lighters in the shape of cars; both the famed MG racers Magic Midget and Montlhéry Midget were so honored. And picnic cases were supplanted by traveling bar sets for the limousines of the well-heeled.

In the 1960s, Sir Malcolm Campbell's son Donald was a keen Dunhill customer who not only owned one of the company's prized "Aquarium" table lighters decorated with an image of his Proteus-Bluebird record-breaker, but also was found with a Dunhill lighter in his pocket when his body was recovered

THE EXCELSIOR MOTOR CAR:
ALWAYS
Magnificent

Whenever Belgian-made automobiles are discussed, the worldwide celebrity of the Minerva usually begins the conversation. Even so, Minerva had a rival in the Excelsior, which could be more exclusive and exotic, with an added racing heritage. The personality differences of the two marques may be attributed to geography – Excelsior was built inland, on the outskirts of the Belgian capital, in comparison to Minerva's factory in the port city of Antwerp.

BY BROOKS T. BRIERLEY

The Excelsior story begins in 1903, when a young twenty-something Belgian engineer, Arthur de Coninck, established a company with a name implying accomplishment, "Compagnie Nationale Excelsior," to build automobiles at 4-6 Avenue de Tervueren in Brussels. His first car, introduced in January 1904, was technically an assembled vehicle built around French-made Aster engines, with one-, two- and four-cylinder configurations.

Excelsior's first success came in 1907, with a four-cylinder model entirely built in-house. It was given the name Adex, created from selecting four letters in Arthur de Coninck Excelsior. The Adex name continued to be part of the Excelsior identity until the end, although its use varied as part of the brand (just after World War I, the car was called Adex-Excelsior) or a model designation.

In 1910 the firm moved to the former premises of the failed Belgica car in Zaventem, on the northeast side of Brussels. A new six-cylinder model gave the Excelsior motor car its final form.

Excelsior's prewar representative for "Great Britain and the Colonies" was H.M. Hobson, Ltd., in London, at 16 Pall Mall, SW. One British car magazine reported "only" two models were offered (given the dealer's name, the comment may have been subtle Hobson's Choice humor). One was a four-cylinder 14-20hp model (displacing 2938 cc); the other, a 20-30hp six-cylinder model with 4407 cc. Both engines had identical bore and stroke measurements (85x130), simplifying their manufacture. The four was set on a 119-inch wheelbase chassis, with a compact 162-inch length. British four-cylinder chassis prices for 1913 were 300 pounds, with a complete car beginning at 375 pounds. The six-cylinder model used a 128½-inch wheelbase, making a 172½-inch length. British prices were 435 pounds for the chassis, with complete cars beginning at 510 pounds. By comparison, a 20-30hp four-cylinder Fiat chassis sold for 515 pounds. At the same time, a complete Ford Model T could be purchased in England for 135 pounds.

Just before World War I, Excelsior entered a series of speed competitions. Two four-cylinder cars were in

Josef Christiaens at the wheel during preparations for the Indianapolis 500 race in May 1914. The Excelsior is stopped in front of the foreign-car garage, located outside turn two of the track.

the 31-car 1911 Grand Prix de France. They made a modest showing. One car, driven by a fellow named Langlois, did not finish, but a second, driven by de Woelmont, took 11th place of the 12 cars finishing.

A four-cylinder Excelsior was one of 57 entries in the second annual (1912) Monte Carlo Rallye, also known at the time as the Monaco Rallye, depending on which automotive magazine was being read. Langlois was again the driver. He set out from Brussels, driving a total distance of 1340 kilometers. His average speed of 22.3 kph was midway between the highest average of 28.5 km/h, in a Durkopp driven from Berlin, and

This handsome limousine was D'Ieteren Freres body no. 2488, made for the Belgian King Albert I, photo dated 1920.

11.8 kph in an Opel that also departed from Berlin. The Excelsior did not finish well – the exact result was not published in English press – while a Belgian rival, Metallurgique, came in sixth. European winter weather combined with these cars' vintage to create a slow-paced Rallye: ninth place was won driving an average of slightly less than 17 km/h (not quite 11 mph)!

Josef Christiaens is the name most associated with

Excelsior's racing history. He was an engineer – training said to provide him with a certain mechanical sympathy – who had worked in the racing departments of Darracq and Vivinus. After winning the 1909 Liedekerke Cup, the nature of his competitiveness changed, and he took up flying at Henry Farman's school. When he returned to automobile competition, he joined Excelsior. Christiaens began with a flourish,

establishing world records at Brooklands for the 850ci class, including 108 mph for the flying kilometer.

Another example of Christiaens' early accomplishments was a point-to-point run in June 1913, when he broke the speed records from Brussels to St. Petersburg, Russia, in a 30-36hp six-cylinder racer. Reflecting Excelsior equipment practice, the car was fitted with Palmer cord tires that were thicker and bulkier than other tires and considered more durable. The car left Brussels on Wednesday, May 21, at 5 p.m. and arrived in St. Petersburg at 7 a.m. that Saturday. Numerous stops reduced the net running time to 37 hours, with an average speed slightly in excess of 50 mph. Christiaens sold the winning car in St. Petersburg to Russian driver H. Slupsky, who regularly raced it in Russia.

The following month two Excelsiors were entered in the Grand Prix de France, 29 laps totaling 917 kilometers through the countryside and village streets in the vicinity of Amiens. The Excelsiors began the race inauspiciously. Fog delayed the early morning start of the race; the Excelsiors were among the cars having trouble starting up. Each entry left at one-minute intervals. Christiaens' Excelsior I carried No. 5 identification, indicating his starting time was 5:35 a.m. L.G. Hornsted drove Excelsior II as No. 11, with a 5:41 departure. Once underway, both Excelsiors slipped into motoring press obscurity; surviving reports of the race focus on the battle for first place, which neither Excelsior was able to do.

Eleven of the 20 cars finished, including both Excelsiors. Christiaens came in eighth, with Hornsted 11th (a Peugeot was first). Excelsior appears to have relied on a tortoise-and-hare driving strategy to avoid the stresses and risks of top speeds. Even so, that did not prevent either Excelsior from experiencing performance issues.

Specifications of these Excelsior race cars, such as four-speed gearbox, Bosch ignition and spark plugs, Houdaille shock absorbers and Claudel carburetors, often matched competitors'. Even so, the English Palmer cord tires and Adex wheels were unique to the Grand Prix Excelsiors racing that year. Everyone else used Dunlop, Pirelli and Continental tires with Rudge-Whitworth detachable wire wheels, reported to have a new pattern that year, or Goodyear steel wheels.

The effort required to participate in these competitions suggests Excelsior was becoming an increasingly important automotive manufacturer; yet, 1913 production was said to be a modest 250 chassis. Adex wheel and suspension production appears also to have been an important part of the business, which raises the question of whether Excelsior's component manufacture was on a scale large enough to make the motor car's objective – or at least one of them – to be a rolling advertisement for its parts.

Excelsior also competed in the United States just before World War I. Christiaens and his six-cylinder Excelsior, given extra presence with a shapely, polished radiator shell and a thick line of vents indented

into the top of the hood, was one of a number of European entries in the 1914 500-mile International Sweepstakes at the Indianapolis Motor Speedway. This was the time when European cars were winning significant races here. Christiaens' Atlantic crossing was news, too, being among two Delages, a Peugeot, an English Sunbeam and a German-made Bugatti (Alsace became part of France after the treaty of Versailles in 1919), also competing at Indianapolis, that sailed on *La Provence* from Cherbourg on May 9, 1914. That year, Christiaens was sixth at Indianapolis with a 6:27:24 time. That was only four minutes behind Barney Oldfield's Stutz, yet nearly half an hour slower than the winning 6:03:45 time of the Delage.

POSTWAR

W orld War I took a great toll on Excelsior. The Germans occupied the Zaventem factory for most of the war, commandeering the Indianapolis 500 racer in the process and

Top: D'Ieteren Freres' body no. 4107 was a stunning-looking sport sedan of Weymann construction made in late 1927 for a Mr. Nierenstein. It is trimmed in a bold style usually associated with Isotta-Fraschini. Above: D'Ieteren Freres transformable body no. 2738 was built for Mr. J. Cornet in January 1922.

reportedly removing much of the equipment. The war did not stop Christiaens from racing; he returned to Indianapolis for the 1916 500-mile run, driving a Sunbeam. Once the war ended, there was hope things would return quickly to normal. As the factory concentrated on reviving production, racing was deferred, so Christiaens continued his Sunbeam relationship. Early in February 1919, he met what has become a tragic, too-common racing fate; he was killed in his car as he sought to avoid hitting a bystander during a test run.

Later that year, Excelsior reentered the automobile market. The new six-cylinder chassis was a mix of contemporary and established technical features. The prewar motor, cast in two blocks, was rated at 25-40 hp. New were four-wheel brakes connected diagonally, and a stabilizer on the back axle combined with a cantilevered rear suspension to minimize body roll. Also new was a very compact forked torque tube. One review pointed out how this compactness facilitated equipping the cars with either right- or left-hand drive, illustrating Excelsior's export ambitions.

In October 1922, Excelsior introduced a new model, powered by a large 5332cc six-cylinder monoblock engine. Fitting three carburetors on one model hinted that Excelsior would soon be competing again. M. de Coninck found new racing heroes in Andre Dils and Nicolas Carels. In late May 1923, two Excelsiors were entered in the first Le Mans Grand Prix d'Endurance. The weather was not good, mixing wind and rain with some hail and suggesting the results would include surprises. One Excelsior, labeled No. 1, driven by Dils and Nicholas Carels, came in first in its class (5001cc –8000cc displacement) with an average speed of 80.556 km/h for the 1,933 kilometers. The second racer, labeled No. 2, was driven by Gonzaque Lecoreul and F. Flaud. It ran a bit slower, averaging 76.8 km/h. Knowing that the two Excelsiors were the only cars in their class should not take too much away from the results – having their own category in a race like Le Mans was clever promotion.

Other contests, such as the Coupe Baillot (Boulogne) that year and the following year's Circuit de Belgique, saw Excelsiors producing Josef Christiaens-like results – finishing in middle places. That may have affected passenger car marketing. Excelsiors were still not shown at the October 1924 annual London automobile show, at the Olympia. It was not until 1925 or so that they appeared abroad in any quantity. By 1926, there

This attractive D'Ieteren-bodied convertible coupe was photographed on Jan. 11, 1927, in Belgium's Esplanade du Cinquantenaire. D'Ieteren Freres records catalogue it as racing car body no. 3927, made for a Mr. Weimann.

was a small showing of them in Spanish registrations; none were in Madrid, but a single car was in Barcelona, compared to four Minervas, and four cars in Seville, where there were 21 Minervas.

Excelsior only built chassis, setting the stage to be a showcase of luxury coachwork. And what an impressive job was done! Belgian coachbuilders such as D'Ieteren Freres, Snutsel, Vesters et Neirinck and Van den Plas were the primary suppliers, of course, but the British Maythorn and the French Binder firms were also making bodies for the cars. A comprehensive record of D'Ieteren bodies survives in the D'Ieteren Gallery archives in Brussels, including all 123 bodies that firm built on Excelsior chassis.

A very interesting example of D'Ieteren's work involves Hibbard & Darrin. Until the late 1920s, Hibbard & Darrin, with no manufacturing capabilities of its own, had bodies built on contract by different Belgian coachbuilders. Surviving records indicate D'Ieteren Freres built two Hibbard designs for the Excelsior chassis with the 142-inch wheelbase. One was a two-window, four-passenger sedan, D'Ieteren Freres body no. 3029, and the other a landaulet, body no. 3071. As Hibbard & Darrin was D'Ieteren's client, the cars' ultimate owners are not given in those records. Their identification numbers indicate build dates about 1923.

One of the most interesting coachbuilt body styles of the early 1920s was the transformable developed by the French bodybuilder Gustave Baehr, also known as

Above right: A look inside D'Ieteren Freres body no. 3793, an imperial limousine delivered in January 1927 to a Mr. Cassel. Above: D'Ieteren Freres body no. 3029 was designed by Hibbard & Darrin.

the proprietor of the Saint-Didier Automobiles business in Paris. D'Ieteren Freres licensed the design in 1922; it became a series-custom body used on many different chassis. Baehr's design used a series of removable windows and pillars, stowed in a trunk behind the rear seat, plus a foldable roof. Soon there were Excelsior examples; a restored 1924 transformable, originally sold in Barcelona, Spain, survives in the D'Ieteren Gallery in Brussels.

The most famous Excelsior in North America was a limousine reportedly made for King Albert I of Belgium. It is not clear how much of its story is true and how much is lore, but we do know the car existed. The story is told that the king helped construct the bulletproof body in his own workshop and used the car during the war. After the Armistice, the Excelsior was said to be given to a Belgian banker, Alfred Loewenstein. The second owner's sudden death in 1928 brought the car to New York City, where Larry Fay bought it. His own notoriety added to the Excelsior's then-famous armor plate. Rudy Vallee was one of the celebrities who received mention in the press for riding with Fay in the car. Then Fay gave the Excelsior to his business partner, the movie star and nightclub hostess Texas Guinan. A conspicuous symbol of the Roaring Twenties' excess, Guinan's headline-grabbing lifestyle added a flamboyant side to the Excelsior image. The regular Prohibition legal problems of her nightclub friends had the car seen at getting-out-of-jail parties. Guinan used the limousine regularly until her death in late 1933. That December, during the auction of her estate in New York City, the Excelsior had trouble finding bids. At the last minute, a dealer bought the car for only $80. In April 1934, the Excelsior made headlines again. *Time* magazine reported it was in Halifax, Nova Scotia, being put on board the Cunard liner *Scythia*, bound for Liverpool, as the car began a return to Belgium, to be added to a museum of King Albert's memorabilia. However, the

An elegant convertible Victoria from D'Ieteren Freres. The body identification, no. 4141, indicates a production date of early 1928.

The Brussels-based D'Ieteren Gallery owns this restored 1924 transformable model (also on p. 34).

Once owned by Don Russell, this touring Excelsior is now in the hands of Jacques Vander Stappen. According to the current owner, it was bodied by Lebaron. Vander Stappen also owns a 1925 Maythorn-bodied roadster.

rate radiator, placed underneath the water radiator, for engine oil. Controlling the temperature of the oil was considered an important operating issue. The Model C was set on a short 130-inch wheelbase chassis, enhancing handling and improving the power-to-weight ratio. It included a four-speed transmission.

The Model C's introduction coincided with the revival of Belgian racing at Spa. Post-World War I problems delayed the first postwar run of the 24-hour Spa race, called Grand Prix de Belgique, a touring car grand prix. Excelsior's postwar debut there came in the July 1925 race. Two identical Excelsiors were entered. Leon Elscamp drove entry No. 4; Andre Dils drove No. 7. Elscamp came in third; Andre Dils did not finish because of a timing gear problem.

Excelsior's interest in racing never waned. The company's new manager, Raoul de Thier, organized an extensive competitive schedule that included three teams of drivers. The trio's first display was at the September 1926 Circuit des Routes Pavees, also known as the Grand Prix de Lille, in northeast France. Nicholas Carel's Excelsior took first place; Andre Pisart's took fifth. The company gained a new dealer at this time, too, when Pisart added Excelsiors to his Fiat showroom on Brussels' Boulevard de Waterloo.

More significant racing results were made during Excelsior's last time at Spa in May 1927. Raoul de Thier must have sensed the importance of the moment — three cars were readied for the contest. Excelsior took the two best honors. Robert Senechal with Nicholas Carels took first prize; the car driven by Andre Dils and Jacques Ledure placed second.

An Adex stabilizer improved the suspension of underslung cantilever springs in the rear and long flat semielliptic front springs, preventing side sway. Adex also provided the Excelsior's basic mechanical braking system. There was a debate at the time about the merits of modest versus strong brakes, which Excelsior, among others, solved by equipping its cars with a two-brake system, the second stronger set being the impressive Dewandre servo-mechanical brakes. This double-brake system was a period safety ideal.

Excelsior's renewal revived interest in selling the

museum was never built. The Excelsior's subsequent whereabouts have yet to be revealed.

REVIVAL

Excelsior renewed its racing heritage in the mid-1920s, with Arthur de Coninck continuing to run the business. They influenced the passenger cars, with the racing specifications becoming one of two lines of passenger cars. Save for various refinements, these two models were sold for the remainder of the decade. The basic model was named Model B, or Adex B Tourisme in Belgium, originally with a 30-60hp 5344cc side-valve engine with a single carburetor and a three-speed transmission. It was set on a long 142-inch wheelbase. The Model C, or Adex-Sport in Belgium, was the Model B powerplant enhanced with a shaft-driven overhead camshaft, operating inclined valves, and three Zenith carburetors, producing 100 bhp. This reflected the European preference for using carburetors to create more power instead of enlarging engine displacement, mitigating automobile taxes based on displacement. The Model C included a sepa-

cars in the United States. The public introduction appears to have been a Fleetwood close-coupled sedan body, painted in two shades of gray, shown among pages of avant-garde subjects in *Vanity Fair* magazine in 1926. It was an unusually restrained design; at the time, European examples of Excelsior coachwork included dramatic colorings and design. The representative in New York City, Excelsior Motor Car Co., was located near Manhattan's Broadway-based automobile row, at 119 W. 57th St.; a service station was not too far away at 419 W. 55th St. (addresses better known for identifying Isotta Motors' Isotta Fraschini facilities). Sadly, in the peak of the 1920s boom, Excelsior's technical points were not competitive. The firm's changing direction in Europe made sure they were gone from the American market by 1929. Even so, owners were not immediately abandoned; Isotta Fraschini's New York service station remained open into 1933.

In the late 1920s, Hayward Automobiles, Ltd., maintained Excelsior's London showroom in the West End, at Kingsbury House, King Street, St. James' SW The service station was on Kimberley Road, Willesden Lane, NW.

Hayward made small but stunning exhibits at the annual London automobile show, Olympia. In October 1926, the stand included a bare chassis revealing, among other features, Excelsior's unique Adex stabilizer. A completed town car-cabriolet was also there. Both body and fenders were painted a light green, with the interior in brown. An extraordinary brown touring car, with the body edged in wood trim, rounded out the display. These impressive cars emphasized the automobile as a craft, which makes them so interesting today. However, at the time, that characteristic

foretold both production cost issues – Excelsior was building only 100 chassis per year – and defiance of a market increasingly interested in performance.

CONSOLIDATION

Excelsior's business direction changed significantly in 1927. Arthur de Coninck sold the company to Mathieu Van Roggen, who added the marque to his corporate collection of Belgian automobile manufacturers controlled by Imperia, a builder of midprice cars. Excelsior retained its own identity and construction; there is no evidence of it becoming a badge-engineered Imperia underneath. Yet, the rumored eight-cylinder Excelsior, a model so important to the luxury market at the time, was never built. Instead, there were some fine technical refinements made to existing models. Model B's were now rated at 80 hp.

This new situation changed Excelsior's practice of exporting bare chassis to foreign countries. Now

Above and opposite: More views of Vander Stappen's touring car, in Belgium. Below: 1924 transformable.

Belgian-bodied models were emphasized. While it was more profitable to sell a complete luxury car, rejecting local coachwork challenged many export markets' nationalistic sensitivities. Marques that understood this were more popular; it was one of the reasons Packard did so well abroad. Those that did not lost market share. A graphic example of the issue for Excelsior was seen in England, with its large market for imported luxury cars. As the 1928 reviews began – the English car magazines often did detailed test drives as well as general stories – a change in approach became obvious. What had been highly complimentary reviews, such as the 1926 James Young boattailed convertible, helped with the taillight held in place by a silver monkey seated on the car's fuel tank, came with titles such as "A Car of Contradictions." It reviewed a Belgian-bodied car. Positive characteristics, such as the dual braking system, were lost in a discussion of their service issues and a criticism of Belgian roads.

Another Excelsior review that year impassionedly recited specifications about the car, adding pro forma photos of models with little comment.

Even so, those reports always included an unconditionally positive sense of Excelsior's special coachwork. It was both attractive and practical, whether one noticed an Excelsior was handsome and especially comfortable or that ventilation issues were well done. Because Excelsiors were virtually an individual design, each car added something to the image.

One of the Sport C cars sold in England during this time had a dramatic Snutsel torpedo body. The hood and cowl were polished aluminum, with the body painted crimson lake. The interior was upholstered in black. High-crowned fenders and mounting twin spare tires behind the trunk added touches of old Europe. Sleeker, more contemporary designs were seen, too. One coachbuilder may have come closest to going over the top with a splendid-looking faux cabriolet coupe, also on the Sport chassis, painted a single pale color. It included unpainted metal-edged fenders, polished chrome wheel covers and the radiator screen made popular by Isotta-Fraschini.

In January 1929, a grand business scheme was announced by Belgian hotel magnate J. Marquet. American automobiles in all price classes were threatening European manufacturers with better features produced at lesser costs; worse, many established European firms were no longer profitable. As one of those marques built more as a craft than a manufactured product, Excelsior was especially vulnerable to this changing automobile market. Many luxury automobiles had begun adopting more mass-production-like construction details, such as replacing hand-hammered aluminum bodies with pressed steel ones – one of the signs emphasizing that Excelsior and many of its European luxury competitors were losing buyer interest. Marquet's plan was to combine all Belgian automobile companies with Mercedes-Benz, Voisin and Citroen, plus unnamed British and Italian companies, forming a European version of General Motors. It sounded promising. Somehow this plan unraveled; perhaps it was Citroen's public rejection of the idea. Whatever, the consolidation never took place.

Instead, in early 1929, the Excelsior business went through a painful rationalization. Operations were moved to Liege – it is not clear if the final chassis was built there or at Zaventem – with production stopped later in the year. The marque technically remained in business, but the end of racing revealed the determination to shut down all activity. These last cars remained stunning, set on the long 142-inch wheelbase chassis with the venerable 30-80hp six-cylinder overhead valve engine.

By June 1930, it was clear that Excelsior-Imperia continued to weaken from the dual strain of increased worldwide competition and the financial pressures of the beginning world Depression. In a final attempt to reverse the decline, the firm began a vigorous public outcry for protectionist measures to bar American automobile imports into Belgium. By then, the combined production of the Excelsior-Imperia group was only 4,000 cars – not two-thirds of Pierce-Arrow production in the United States. Belgian automotive trade statistics were reported to reveal one car was exported for every five to 10 imports. The imbalance in trade with the United States was especially lopsided; in 1929, 17,000 American cars were sold in Belgium with only 150 Belgian cars imported (most of these would have been Minervas). However compelling these numbers were, the draconian measures needed to correct them were too difficult to make in time to save the Excelsior brand (its Imperia relation survived by licensing German Adler technology).

The marque's finale was at the December 1930 Brussels Automobile Show. It was a testament to the Excelsior image – and to the changes wrought by the worldwide Depression – that it could appear to be in business a year after production shut down. The official end came in 1932. The factory continued to be used into the following year for Imperia bodywork, and it survived World War II. Later used as a laundry, it was torn down in the 1960s. The site then became part of a commercial development. The Excelsiorlaan street in the Keiberg industrial park in Zaventem remains as a memorial.

Few Excelsiors survive. In the 1930s, cars that remained in Belgium began to be converted to utility vehicles, the ironic fate of many Classic Era luxury cars, and then were lost. Fortunately, some of the cars exported to far-flung places such as South Africa and Australia by the London agent survive. Others have been in the United States and Spain. More recently, they began returning to Belgium. An Albert I touring car that had been in the United States, a 1925 Maythorn-bodied roadster seen in a 2004 Bonham's auction, and a 1924 transformable sold in Barcelona have also been among them. The Classic Car Club of America recently added the 1925-1932 Albert I models to the official definition of a Classic Car, something that should make them more visible. ◢◑

Museum Manager David Yando (left) and owner Jeff Lane in the Lane Motor Museum's main showroom.

More than Music in Music City
THE LANE MOTOR MUSEUM

Nashville, Tenn., is rife with popular destinations and events: The Grand Ole Opry, Music Row, the Nashville Film Festival, and the Country Music Association's Music Festival, to name just a few. What's also found in "the Athens of the South" is reminiscent of the Tennessee state capital's rich history – the Lane Motor Museum, an assembly of intriguing mobility.

BY TRACY POWELL

Tourism is the name of the game in Nashville, and museum owner Jeff Lane has hedged his bets on his growing and evolving collection of unique models – around 325 at the time of this printing. Amidst the Lane Motor Museum's numerous automobiles are motorcycles, military vehicles and trucks, as well as models that defy categorization. In short, Lane's collection is eclectic and vast.

From a young age, Lane was nudged in the direction of the automotive hobby. If genetics have anything to do with it, perhaps he got it from his car-loving father. The elder Lane opened an automotive supply business in Michigan in 1958, opening young Jeff's eyes to old MGs, Jaguars and other makes and models.

"We had a workshop attached to the house next to the garage where we worked on restoration projects, the first one I think was an MG TF," Lane said. "My dad got attached to MGs when he was in Germany in the U.S. Army in the 1950s. He bought a new MG TF in 1954, brought it back to Detroit, drove it for about a

Jeff Lane (above, at the Glenmoor Gathering in Canton, Ohio, with a 1928 Martin Aerodynamic) is intentional in his efforts to keep his vehicles in front of enthusiasts, both inside and outside his museum. Left: Lane's "moving crew" lifts a Peel from its transporter.

year, and then got married. He realized after driving it for that long that, one, it wasn't a very good car, and, two, it's a two-seater and not a good family car. So he got rid of it."

Following the MD TF experience as a daily driver, Lane's father yearned to get an MG again, this time in

the 1960s. "That's when he got back into older cars," says Jeff. "And I worked on them alongside him. In the summer he would go to work during the day, and he would tell me, 'Here's this car, and do this, this and this today.' So I would spend the day working on the car. That's where it started for me and it sort of blossomed from there."

"Blossom" is an apt word: Because his dad was an MG fan, it was only natural for Jeff to start out with a love for British models. At one time, the Lane family had seven MGs when Jeff was young, and members of the family would attend meets around the country. When Lane was 12 and working on a car, his father asked what Jeff would like for Christmas.

"I had been working on his car for a couple of years at that time, and I said I'd like to have an MG of my own – never thinking that would ever come to pass.

He ended up giving me an MG TF for Christmas, but it was in pieces. The deal was: If I restored it, the car was mine. Of course, I restored it."

Lane was, of course, too young too drive at that time. He grew up in the small town of Romeo, north of Detroit, with a population of about 10,000. And in small towns, formalities are often waived for the sake of neighborliness.

"There was one lady who did all the drivers' tests and ran all the plates in that town," Lane said. "She always wanted to ride in my dad's car, and one time he told her that I would be getting my license soon, and when I did I would come down and she could get a ride in my car. So we went down in my car, she got in, and she wanted to go to her neighbor's house, which was about a mile and a half away. We drove over there, returned to the office, and then she gave me my license."

across the country and Europe. We either go to someone, or they come to us and say, 'You've got a weird taste for cars – I have just the car for you.'"

It is this taste that makes the Lane Museum stand out from others.

"The very nature of the collection is its oddity," said Greg Coston, Lane's full-time restorer and conservator. "There's a lot of mechanical oddity," such as the Dymaxion reproduction that was under construction in Coston's shop during our visit.

Lane's U.S.-built Martin Stationette is a prime example of this oddity. It is a hand-built, three-wheeled automobile purchased from the AACA Museum. It had to be rebuilt from the "tire treads up" according to Yando. "A number of craftsmen had to do different types of work to finally get it ready for Amelia Island, and it took longer than a year of pretty arduous work."

Having so many one-of-a-kind cars presents challenges that few usually face. Just about every car Lane's crew has worked on recently has been a lesson in self-education. "We've had to figure it out ourselves,"

Lane's unique collection of cars is intriguing and fun to look at while static in the museum, and they're also exciting to watch in motion. Living history, left to right: A crowd favorite, the air-propelled 1932 Helicron; a 1964 Amphicar taking to the water; driving the obstacle course at the museum's 2007 Microcar Day; Lane at the wheel of one of the collection's several Citroens.

A Collection on the Move

Since its opening in October 2003, the Lane museum has not been a static collection. In fact, vehicles are rarely in the same spot for any extended period of time. They are being driven, trucked to a show, taken to the shop for more restoration or duplication, or simply rotated out and replaced with a different model from the basement.

"The vast majority of cars come through Jeff one way or another," said museum manager David Yando. "We belong to 50-60 car clubs all over the world, so we get car club newsletters. We also travel to concours

Yando said. Yet none have proven too much to tackle.

"If I thought any of them was tough to work on, I'd have real trouble," Coston said. "There are times when it would be nice to have old Fords or Chevies, mass-produced models with parts that are easy to come by. But that would be really boring. A few years ago I worked on a car called the Houston Rocket, which I

The majority of the Lane collection is arranged by country: Austria, Czechoslovakia, France, Germany, Great Britain, Italy, Japan, Netherlands, Sweden and the United States. Visitors learn how similar – and different – vehicles are from one part of the world to another, and why. The largest Czechoslovakian collection outside Europe is housed here.

was enthusiastic about because it had a Ford drivetrain. I thought I could get parts and we were home free. The first thing you do when you get a vehicle in is take everything off of it to see what you need, so you can start looking for it early in the process.

"Come to find out, this car was a V8 60, which, as it turned out, required parts that [were] somewhat harder to find. So some of the American stuff, the things that you would think [are] easy to get supplies for, can turn

around and not be so easy."

The efforts at the museum do not stop at automobiles.

"Jeff had been saying he wanted to build up the military vehicles," Yando said. "I asked him what he wanted, maybe a tank. But he wanted something unusual. So I found a Lark – an amphibious military transport – on eBay as a joke. Next thing I knew, here it was."

ALL ABOUT ACCESSIBILITY

It wasn't until about 10 years ago that Lane had very many vintage cars. Up to that time, he spent much of his spare time racing in SCCA. Lane decided to slow down his racing activities, and that's when the collector car hobby bit in a more serious way. At one point approximately eight years ago, Lane real-

have access to the cars, to be able to see them. The museum was the perfect way to do that."

Space grew from 15,000 square feet to 140,000 square feet when Lane moved the cars into the present building, a former bakery. What seemed like a huge number of cars at the time barely filled up the new exhibit floor. A 60,000-square-foot basement under the building comes in handy for storage. This allows about 125 cars to be displayed on the main exhibit floor, which is around 45,000 square feet.

Even with that much space, with such an eclectic collection, the question became: How do you arrange them? The majority of the collection is grouped by country, yet other groups, such as microcars and race cars, necessitated their own areas. Fortunately there was enough elbow room for "outside-the-box" groupings.

Microcars are always an attraction at shows, "I think because most Americans don't know anything about microcars," Lane said. "You see some that are basic, crude things and others that are somewhat stylistic. The microcar guys tried everything because there weren't any rules except to make them cheap and efficient. There were a lot of oddball things that were tried … it was a wide-open world, and I think they came out with cars that were interesting – you could call them whacky, too. Sometimes the ideas worked, sometimes they didn't."

Lane has no expansion plans at the moment, likely because a 50,000-square-foot attached indoor parking garage is not filled yet.

ized he had about 75 cars in five different buildings.

"People around town would see cars like the Amphicar and they would find out that I had a bunch of cars, which led to requests for tours," Lane said. "Sometimes I would take people through the different buildings, which were basically garages crammed with models. People would always want to see a certain car, which was either at my house or in a building that didn't have great access, so they couldn't see everything. My thought at that point was I either had to stop collecting cars or I needed to put them in – what I call – a proper entity. Part of my desire was for people to

The majority of the vehicles in the Lane museum were built in the 1950s through the 1970s, although some are as old as the 1920s and as new as 2000. Visitors are introduced to a broad cross-section of vehicles, with more than 45 marques representing Asia, Europe, and North and South America. The floor plan is laid out logically, allowing for easy sauntering around the sections.

Also at the museum is a comfortable and spacious research library, where enthusiasts can learn more about some of the mostly European marques represented in the adjacent showroom.

"With 125 cars we have enough synergy there to rotate about four cars a month," Lane said, "so if someone comes once a year they see a substantial turnover of cars they haven't seen before. We want to have enough to continually change what is being presented."

The museum also has a meeting room, capable of seating 75, that can be rented. The room has a sink and refrigerator, but not a full catering service. The exhibit area is also rented for evening events. Local schools use the space for fundraising events, and the local operas has also rented space. Once a year, Bridgestone brings its engineers from around the world to the facility.

Visitors will notice a large Tatra collection, which fits in well with the museum's uniquely global approach to displaying motorcars. More recently is a push for motorcycles of many eras.

"We're not active on the auction circuit, because what we're looking for are models that expand our core collections; one core collection consists of microcars, another is Tatra cars, and yet another is propeller-powered cars," Lane said. "Most of those are pretty obscure. So, instead of hitting auctions, we spend more time using connections, such as people in clubs we belong to. They know what we're looking for, and they either hunt us down or we hunt down the cars."

The Lane Museum markets itself on a small budget, a budget that is used judiciously.

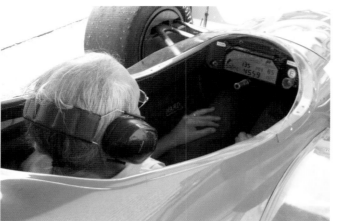

Whether rallying in one of his unique gems or educating crowds on the museum grounds, Jeff Lane is one of the hobby's most dedicated advocates. Museum staff has seen visitor attendance increase at a healthy pace since its opening in 2007.

"We do a little print advertising in some local publications that are geared toward parents of school-children," Yando said. "We do some limited, targeted advertising on Comcast cable television – they have attractively priced 30-second ads. We've not done much on radio lately because it's so hard to impart such a visual thing, but we are discussing doing some things on public radio, on the 'Car Talk' program. We had some success with that in the past."

The museum went through its first year without any marketing, per se, according to Yando. "What little we did was mainly lending out cars to visitor centers and sending press releases. We really did not have that expertise. After about a year, we hired a marketing person who got us started on the right track, and we continue to be doing well. We saw a 200-percent-plus increase in our visitor tally from our first year to 2007."

Through 2008, the Lane Museum welcomed approximately 22,000 visitors. By picking and choosing how to spend its marketing dollars, the museum's staff welcomes about 1,000 people a month, as opposed to 300 a month just a few years ago.

Not bad for any museum, let alone one in a town with so many other destinations clamoring for visitors. AQ

MINI TO THE MAX

Taking Mini-derivatives to Heart

So much has been written and said about the Mini the past 50 years, you would think there was nothing new to add. However, the greatest small car in the world has brought life to numerous derivatives and specials, many of which have remained in obscurity.

BY JEROEN BOOIJ

Since it's been 50 years this year that the Mini bounced into the motoring scene, chances are slim you missed the anniversary. In fact, the Mini's story has been told umpteen times, including its 1960s fashion statements and heroic Monte Carlo victories. The 10-foot "brick" that Alec Issigonis, Jack Daniels and the rest of the BMC development engineers brought to life in 1959 has become a bit of a legend itself. But still, a part of the Mini's history never seems to be taken seriously and is therefore much undervalued; it is the enormous influence the great little car had on the kit car industry.

introducing the

BROADSPEED G.T. 2+2

BROADSPEED are proud to present their revolutionary G.T. 2+2, which gives an exciting and unforgettable experience in motoring. These cars are for the motorist to whom driving is an essential part of his day to day life, but who likes to do it with flair and who enjoys the supreme pleasure of a car which gives the ultimate in control and response, combined with the looks of a thoroughbred. Naturally, we have not forgotten the requirements of the racing enthusiast, to whom the word "Broadspeed" is synonymous with the tough and competitive world of international saloon car racing.

In these models lie the culmination of experiments conducted by the top engineers in our competition department and the gruelling test of world famous race tracks.

Don't take our word for it. Come and see for yourself. Admire the gleaming body, the interior, fitted and finished by craftsmen and finally examine the superb engineering and you will understand why Broadspeed are proud to present their . . .

ence. And it didn't take long before streamlined bodies were available. You could buy one from companies such as Ashley Laminates, Speedex Castings or Falcon Shells from under £100 and turn a tired old Austin Seven or Ford Popular, with its straightforward chassis and well-proven power unit, into something that looked somewhat like a C-type Jaguar or Aston Martin DBR1. That most of them rattled, squeaked, leaked and overheated didn't seem to disturb their owners. Brits loved these cheap and eccentric little sports cars. The market proved, in fact, to be so hungry that by the end of the '50s, the choice for body styles was abundant. Any owner of a rusty old Austin or Ford dreaming to convert his mundane sedan into something more exotic could choose from well

Or perhaps we should talk about specialist cars in a cottage industry, as this is a very British affair. As a matter of fact, the market for these limited-production DIY sports cars had reached a peak in the U.K. when the Mini was introduced in August 1959. About a decade earlier, British motoring enthusiasts had started offering cheap sports cars in component form for budding racing drivers. The invention of fiberglass, the new wonder material, undoubtedly had a great influ-

Above: One of presumed 28 Broadspeed GTs built by the Birmingham-based racing stable of the same name. Left: Rare picture of the 1961/62 Butterfield Musketeer.

This Camber GT (left) is the only one of six cars built that came with lightweight shell. It was raced throughout its life (right). The GT's low headlights were found to be illegal just after its launch and the car was redesigned and renamed Maya GT. Not more than another six were built.

over 100 different sleek roadster and coupé bodies. But their downfall was soon to come. In fact, the introduction of the Mini in 1959 spelled the end of these sluggish specials. The Mini was relatively cheap and could outperform and out-handle most of them easily, thanks to its ingenious cone-and-trumpet suspension setup. It didn't take the enthusiasts long to find out that Issigonis' baby proved to be a terrific base for their beloved specials. What could be fun in a heavy, steel-body shell could be even better in a lightweight fiberglass body. With its two subframes, attached with just eight bolts each on the Mini's steel body to locate complete power train and suspension, the Mini's mechanicals perfectly lent themselves to the dreams of the self-appointed car designer. A new generation of specialist cars was underway.

LONDON'S RACING CAR SHOW

While the Beatles and the Rolling Stones dominated the charts, sports car enthusiasts with a limited budget were exploring the U.K. scrap yards to find bits and pieces to build up Mini Marcos, Mini Jems or Mini-based Terrapin race cars. According to *Cars and Car Conversions* magazine, it all began somewhere in 1960, "when a keen lad whose name we can't remember turned up at, we think, Silverstone with an enterprising but ugly two-seater sports car based on the dear old Mini. This was a one-off, a private venture with no thoughts of series production." The car in question was never seen again,

but the market for Mini-based specials and derivatives soon mushroomed.

GTs, coupés, roadsters and fun cars: the Mini proved to be a terrific base for some of the world's most imaginative vehicles. On the last day of 1961, the first two Mini-derivatives were launched at the Racing Car Show in London's Royal Horticultural Halls. On stand 18, the Butterfield Engineering Company showed its Butterfield Musketeer. The two-seat coupé was designed by 21-year-old Richard Butterfield, who'd given up his horticulture study to set up a car designing company in his father's nursery. The Musketeer's aluminium body was hand-beaten by coachbuilders Williams and Pritchard of North London and was finished just in time to have the car assembled for the show.

Richard Butterfield had kept as much as possible of the original Mini's mechanicals: "I wanted to take

One of the very few successful designs for a Mini derivative came from Jack Hosker, who styled the GTM (Grand Touring Mini) and teamed up with Bernard Cox. This is an early Cox GTM.

advantage of the handling characteristics and simplicity of the original car. Simplicity was important because I had only limited engineering experience." Butterfield bolted the Mini's subframes together with two longitudinal tubes with welded cross members. The front-engine configuration was retained, and by moving the radiator to the front of the car, it came with a relatively low nose. Production cars were to have fiberglass bodies and were offered from £848. Meanwhile, on the other side of the halls complex, at stand 73, Morgan tuner and racer Christopher Lawrence's company LawrenceTune Engines Ltd. (see *AQ* 46-1) showed its prototype of the Deep Sanderson 301. Like the Musketeer, the Deep Sanderson's aluminium body was done by Williams & Pritchard's and it, too, was to become available in fiberglass kit form. The main difference was in the layout as this car had its Mini engine placed behind driver and passenger. The show guide blurb said: "The car evolved directly from our last Formula Junior car and is of very advanced design. Suspension is all independent by Lawrence

trailing link; engine is 1,000cc transverse mounting; brakes are disc on the front and drums on the rear. The car is primarily for road use and will be sold in kit form at a very low price."

But road use or not – unlike the Butterfield Musketeer that was just raced once – the little 301 was promoted heavily in racing. It even took on the might of Jaguars, Ferraris and other much bigger machinery in classic endurance races such as the 500 kilometers of the Nürburgring and the Le Mans 24 Hours. In 1963, a Deep Sanderson 301 was entered in the famous 24-hour race, driven by Lawrence himself and co-piloted by Chris Spender. With its 998cc Downton-tuned engine, the car did well but was excluded because it had been behind on minimum average at midnight after Spender had slid it into a sandpit. The next year, the team returned with two 1,295cc-engined 301s. One was driven by Lawrence and Gordon Spice, a second by Jim Donnely and Huw Braithwaite, who crashed it during practice. Lawrence and Spice reputedly clocked 148 mph on

the Mulsanne straight in the other car, but when the oil pump broke after four hours, they, too, had to give up.

MINIS AT LE MANS

The Deep Sanderson was not the only Mini-derivative that made it to the sacred grounds of Le Mans. There was also the more successful Mini Marcos GT, a tiny terror launched by Marcos Cars in 1965 to broaden its range of bigger sports cars with a fashionable and cheap Mini-based sports car. At a very low £199, the "Son of Marcos" came as an easy-to-fabricate fiberglass monocoque shell to be finished off with the running gear and subframes from any Mini. According to the advertisements, customers could build the front-wheel-drive car in 15 to 20 hours without specialist knowledge or tooling. One of these customers was the professional deep-sea diver Jean-Claude Hrubon from Paris. He built a car with a 1287 Cooper S-engine and raced it at Monthléry, where

with the build quality of the French privateers' car. Marsh said, "I had nothing to do with the preparation of the car and was horrified when I saw it. I didn't think it would last a lap." But it did, and in fact it came home 15th overall and was the first British car to finish the race that year. Marsh entered an aerodynamically altered works car for the 24-hour race of the next year that managed a cool 141 mph at Mulsanne straight. Unfortunately, it didn't finish because of a broken timing gear. But by then the Mini Marcos was selling well, and an Mk2 version was available.

Then there was the Unipower GT, masterminded by Elva racing team manager Ernie Unger and freelance designer Val Dare-Bryan at Goodwood in 1963. The car had a space frame and independent wheel suspension; it used Mini uprights, modified Mini suspension arms, coil springs and a Mini engine, placed just behind the driver. The striking body was designed by a Ford stylist who wished to remain anonymous because he'd drawn the car when his bosses thought he was working on the GT40. The project was backed by Tim Powell, whose company Universal Power Drives manufactured forklift trucks and mechanical winches and could do with an image boost. Named as the Mini Miura in the motoring press, it was well received, but development of the car turned out to be a problem.

With production finally in full swing, Powell sold the company in 1968 to 22-year-old playboy and racing driver Piers Weld-Forester. Weld-Forester moved production to London and launched the Unipower GT Mk2. He began to concentrate on a comprehensive racing publicity campaign and had three lightweight works cars built. One was entered in the Targa Florio in June 1969. It was air freighted to Sicily, where the car came 12th in practice but was crashed by a mechanic the night preceding the race. Another racer was built to compete in the 24 Hours of Le Mans in July of that year. The car was entered privately by Weld-Forester and was nicknamed "la puce jaune" (the yellow flea) by the French. When it lost a wheel at high speed, there was no serious damage, but later the engine blew up after three hours practicing. And there were similar troubles at the Gran Premio Mugello, the Grand Prix

Above: The Deep Sanderson 301 at Le Mans in 1963. Below: The Deep Sanderson with its dry-sump Mini engine. Below right: The little-known Coldwell GT.

he was asked to have his car driven in the Le Mans 24-hour race of June 1966. Drivers were Jean-Louis Marnat and Claude Ballot-Lena. Marcos-boss Jem Marsh, too, was at Le Mans that year on invitation by *Autocar* magazine and was not particularly pleased

Rear-engined racers: The Landar R7 and the
unique Australian-built Lolita Mk1 (below).

A LUXURIOUS MINI GT

Many more Mini-derivatives were born with a racing career in mind. Beginning with the idea to just build something different, their creators thought racing could be a good means of advertising their products. With cars such as the Mini Marcos, Mini Jem, Cox GTM and Broadspeed GT, this seemed to work; others sold no more then a handful. Six examples of the sharply styled Camber GT, eight Ferrari Dino-inspired Pellandinis, six Maya GTs, and no fewer then 31 strangely proportioned Biotas were brought to life. Others never even made these figures. Production of the Australian Bulanti Mini came to an end when its creator found out how demanding his customers were, with one even asking for an ashtray; no more then three Bulantis materialized. Production

of Denmark and the 12-hour race of Barcelona, all in the 1969 season. The costly racing activities eventually spelled the downfall of the company after only 15 Mk2s were built.

Several Italians came up with a Mini redesign. The "ADO70" (above) was styled by Paul Hughes but built by Michelotti. Right: The unique Zagato Mini Gatto.

of the ultralow Coldwell GT, with its space frame construction, never exceeded four, and the same went for the Fletcher GT and the "miniature Can-Am-racer" Landar R7. Other Mini-based sports cars remained a one-off, such as the pretty Gitane GT, the Boro GT, the Italian ESAP Minimach and Australian Lolita Mk1 and Mk2.

But not all Mini-derivatives were meant to be race-bred. One of the earliest, the Ogle SX1000, actually aimed at the luxury car market. Presented in December 1961 by David Ogle of the design house with the same name, the Mini-based baby GT caused a stir. The SX1000 used all of the Mini's mechanicals, even its complete floor pan, inner wings and part of the bulkhead. It looked completely different, thanks to a striking fiberglass shell. From 1962 on, David Ogle Limited transformed Minis into baby GTs in its Letchworth factory. And thanks to the good design, excellent finish and relatively low price (£550), it was not too hard to find customers for the SX1000. That it cost considerably more to build a car was later revealed by Ogle's then-chairman John Ogier, who said: "It

would have been cheaper to give any customer £300 and told him to go away!" But at Longbridge's British Motor Company, which initially had refused to supply new parts, the apparent success of the Mini-based GT did not go unnoticed. It soon agreed to supply new parts but insisted that the word "Mini" not be used in any promotion. From then on, Ogle supplied brand new cars with the Cooper 997 engine and managed to sell 69 cars worldwide before tragedy struck and David Ogle was killed in a road accident driving one of his own cars.

ZAGATO, MICHELOTTI AND PININFARINA

Some renowned Italian *carrozzerias* had their share in the Mini's derivative story too. Zagato launched its Zagato Mini Gatto in 1961, the same year it came up with the now mega-valued Aston Martin DB4 GT Zagato and Alfa-Romeo Giulietta SZ Coda Tronca. The car was built on the base of a

new Morris Mini Van and came with an aluminium body over its original steel floor. Under the hood, a tuned 998cc Cooper engine came fitted with specially developed Dellorto carburetors. The Mini-Zagato, as the prototype was called, was shown at the Earls Court Motor Show in 1961, where the idea was announced to set up "British Zagato," including a production line, in Kingston-upon-Thames. However, it soon turned out the British Motor Corporation was not particularly happy with the idea. BMC's Lord Stokes claimed it conflicted with his Mini program and did not want to collaborate by supplying cars or parts, thus killing the Mini-Zagato.

Ironically, from 1960 on, BMC worked on a few Mini-derivatives, cooperating with another famous Italian name: Pininfarina. The cars they came up with – internally identifd as ADO34, ADO35 and ADO36 (for Austin Drawing Office) – were Mini-based, but MG-badged roadsters and a GT never saw production. Years later, Michelotti, too, was asked to design and build a Mini-based targa-roof roadster, the ADO70. But because the U.S. was thought to be the main

The Unipower GT was promoted heavily in racing. Three works cars were built to race at the Nürburgring (above) and Le Mans (right), among others. Below: The original Mini sketch by Alec Issigonis.

market, that sharply styled proposal never made it because it was feared the design would not comply with American safety and emissions standards.

The Mini's manufacturers, nevertheless, kept their eyes on the blossoming market of Mini-derivatives. When Barry Stimson launched his Mini Bug in 1970 – an idea he'd come up with when seeing a Myers Manx beach buggy in Canada in 1968 – reactions to the cheap, little Mini-based buggy were good. The car even made it to national television. British Leyland, as the BMC concern now was named, showed an interest, too, and came over to Stimson's humble "factory" to examine the car. Barry Stimson, now resembling an aging rock star, recalls: "They wanted to know all about the stress tests we had put it through. I said we had a fat friend and we got him to bounce up and down on the chassis. If it bent we welded another strut in. We never heard a thing of them anymore.".

ALEC ISSIGONIS' DISLIKE

The blossoming privateers market for Mini roadsters, buggies and coupé derivatives is the main reason why BMC never offered such cars. Apart from that, Sir Alec Issigonis always gave the strong impression he

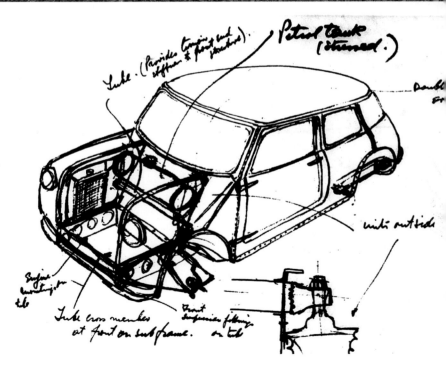

Above: The Ogle SX1000 used the Mini's entire original floor pan. The Mini Marcos (left, at Le Mans) and Mini Jem (below) had their own fiberglass monocoque shells.

disliked these sporty Mini-variants. Marcos-boss Jem Marsh remembers how the Mini's designer disregarded the French-entered Mini Marcos during the Le Mans 24-hour race in 1966. Marsh said, "Alec Issigonis wouldn't even talk about it or look at it, and he left in disgust because it was still running at midnight." Ironically, however, Issigonis too started his motoring career with a Special built by himself and his friend George Dawson on the base of an old Austin Seven, obviously built with the same kind of enthusiasm the designers and builders of all those Mini-derivatives had. Issigonis' "Lightweight Special" actually was his first car to demonstrate the potential of all-independent suspension with rubber springs. And it did well in the hands of its creators just before and after World War II. Much later, Issigonis, who passed away in 1988 at the age of 82, described the car as "a frivolity in my life. It was not so much a design exercise as a means of teaching me to use my hands."

But then, you could say the same of all the specials and derivatives that were born from the Mini. At least they brought some good untold tales to the motoring industry. AQ

JUNIOR JOHNSON
THE LAST
AMERICAN HERO

*F*ew *people might have taken notice when Robert Glen Johnson Jr. was born in the summer of 1931 in Wilkes County, N.C., deep in the heart of the American south and the Great Depression. But once he roared out of Wilkes County to become known simply as Junior Johnson, he never let up.*

BY LEIGH DORRINGTON

Junior Johnson has always been larger than life. Still is. His legend came straight out of the backwoods of North Carolina. He helped make NASCAR the mega-business it is today. He invented drafting. Stood up to Big Bill France. Became the team owner with the most wins in NASCAR's first half century. Brought Winston into Winston Cup, as well as many of the best sponsors still in NASCAR today. Junior Johnson intimidated the Intimidator, Dale Earnhardt. And today he does – legally – what he was sent to prison for, more than 50 years ago.

White-suited writer Tom Wolfe wrote about Junior Johnson for *Esquire* magazine in 1964. In the ensuing years, while NASCAR exploded across America, no one in two generations of overheated writers has told the story better.

Sports Illustrated named Junior Johnson the greatest NASCAR driver of all time on the 50th anniversary of the sport in 1998. As a driver, he won 50 races in

NASCAR's top division during the sport's most dangerous era and retired on top – alive – at the age of 34. As a car owner, he made the mold for today's top teams.

There's no doubt that Junior Johnson has always been his own man.

No example is more telling than a conversation between Junior Johnson and Bill France in 1965. The 1965 racing season was a particularly difficult one for NASCAR. Roots of the problem traced back to 1964, when speeds caused even brave drivers like Buck Baker to say, "It's reached the point at the super-speedways where it's a big relief when a race ends and you're ok, no matter where you finished." Others such as Joe Weatherly, Fireball Roberts and Billy Wade weren't as lucky, losing their lives in racing or testing accidents. NASCAR historian Greg Fielden wrote,

Above: Johnson's first starts in NASCAR's Grand National division were in 1954 in a Cadillac owned by bandleader Paul Whiteman. Top Center: Junior Johnson's first race was at the new North Wilkesboro Speedway in 1949. Right: Johnson shared starts in the Cadillac with close friend Gwyn Staley, shown here together beside Johnson's Oldsmobile in 1955.

Above: Junior Johnson qualified a Mickey Thompson Corvette powered by the 427 "Mystery Motor" for the 1963 NASCAR American Challenge race at Daytona, as well as Ray Fox's No. 3 Chevrolet for the 1963 Daytona 500. Billy Krause drove the Corvette in the race.

"Junior Johnson, regarded as the bravest of the brave, remarked, 'We haven't learned enough to keep the cars handling safely at the speeds we now travel.'"

Rules announced by NASCAR to slow speeds on the track in 1965 included elimination of limited production engines such as Chrysler's 426 Hemi and Ford's Hi-Riser 427. Chrysler immediately announced a boycott of NASCAR. In January, General Motors reinforced an earlier decision not to support racing. Sponsorship as it is known today was virtually nonexistent. Most teams were sponsored by local car dealers or garages, and without some of the top names or factory support, NASCAR was suffering.

Junior Johnson saw this as a good time to ease back and run only selected, high-paying races. When he announced his decision to Bill France Sr., France replied, "You can't do that. NASCAR needs you." The two met for breakfast the next morning to talk. When

Junior insisted that his mind was made up, the conversation seemed to be at a standstill. Then Johnson pointed his fork at his plate and said, "You see that bacon on that plate? And that egg? Well, the pig is committed, but the chicken is just involved. I'm just involved."

CODE OF HONOR

The roots of stock car racing run deep through American history. The production and transportation of illegal whiskey – "moonshine" – came long before the automobile. "At first it was a simple matter of economics," wrote Wolfe in *Esquire*. "The land had a low crop yield, compared to the lowlands, and even after a man struggled to grow his corn, or whatever, the cost of transporting it to the markets from down out of the hills was so great, it wasn't worth it." It was more

profitable to make whiskey from the corn.

Johnson told Wolfe, "I'd say that nearly everybody in a 50-mile radius of here was in the whiskey business at one time or another." Johnson's father, Robert Glen Johnson Sr., was one of the most successful.

"My daddy was always a hard worker," Johnson also told Wolfe. "He always wanted something a little bit better. A lot of people resented that and held it against him, but what he got, he always got it by hard work." As a result, Johnson, his two bothers and three sisters always lived just a little better than others in Wilkes County, although sometimes at the expense of long absences from Johnson Sr. while he served time for making moonshine.

Johnson and his brothers were drawn into the long hours to stoke the fires and keep watch on the stills. And once it came time to transport the finished whiskey to markets, it was a natural that Junior Johnson

Left: Johnson's privately-entered white Ray Fox Chevrolet was the scourge of the 1963 NASCAR season. Right: Junior Johnson also practiced a Kurtis roadster at Indianapolis in 1963 but did not attempt to qualify. This was the last Kurtis built for Indy (note roll cage).

would be drawn to that, too.

According to biographers Tom Higgins and Steve Waid, Junior Johnson started delivering moonshine at 14. He hauled moonshine for his father, for his older brothers and, eventually, for himself. It was largely a game of cat and mouse between the moonshiners and the revenuers who enforced the federal alcohol tax.

"Runners" favored Ford coupes. They modified or replaced the engine, sometimes with a Cadillac or Oldsmobile ohv V8, and installed stronger rear springs and larger wheels and tires to handle the heavier weight of their cargo. The rear seat, if there was one, could be removed to increase space for the whiskey.

"These cars," wrote Wolfe, "were plain on the outside, so they wouldn't attract attention." "But, there was no way you could make it sound like an ordinary car," said Junior Johnson. Wolfe's account has become a classic of American journalism: "God-almighty, that sound in the middle of the night, groaning, roaring, humming down into the hollows, through the clay gulches – yes!" There he goes. Junior Johnson.

Junior Johnson was never caught on the road. But as he became more well known in the emerging sport of NASCAR stock car racing, he became a target of the federal agents. "I was out of the whiskey business, and they knew that, but they was just waiting to catch me on something," he told Wolfe. That something was a simple act of loyalty to his family.

"I had won a race in Oxford, Pa., on a Saturday night," Johnson told an interviewer in 2007. "It was almost daylight when I got home. And my dad asked me to go fire his still up for him, 'cause if you didn't fire up the still and get the smoke away from it before daylight, someone would see it. I didn't think anything about doing what my dad said. There was nobody but me there, and I was firing the still up. I heard something over my shoulder and there was a guy just standing on top of a box just fixin' to jump on my back. He hollered out 'Catch Junior Johnson!' I knew where there was an opening, a gate in the fence, and I was going to have to hit that opening if I was to get away. I missed that opening and I got tangled up in the barbed

wire fence. They caught me."

Junior Johnson was sentenced to two years in the federal penitentiary in Chillicothe, Ohio, where he served 11 months and three days before being released. "But I don't think the true facts of the case justified the sentence I got," he said. "I had never been arrested in my life. I think they [were] punishing me for the past … but it was two or three years I was set back [from racing]. I think I lost the prime of my racing career."

But if Junior Johnson missed the prime of his racing career while he was sitting out those seasons, how does anyone explain what happened next?

JUNIOR JOHNSON'S LEGACY

Generations have been told the story of how Junior Johnson was plowing corn for his father, barefoot behind a mule, when his older brother L.P. came home from the new North

Wilkesboro Speedway to tell him they were having a special race for local boys in their whiskey-hauling cars. Junior put up the mule, got his shoes and went to the track with L.P. and his 1940 Ford Standard. He finished second to his friend Gwyn Staley, but only after a lapped car cut him off late in the race.

Junior became a regular competitor in the Sportsman Division, which was made up mostly of prewar coupes stripped for racing. Bill France Sr. introduced big-band leader Paul Whiteman to Johnson in 1954, and Junior made three starts in Whiteman's Cadillac, sharing the car with Staley. He teamed up with local businessmen Carl Buchanan and Jim Lowe in 1955. Junior Johnson's first Grand National victory came on May 7, 1955, at Hickory Speedway, a four-tenths mile dirt track in Hickory, N.C. He beat 1952 (and 1955) Grand National Champion Tim Flock, who was driving one

of Carl Kiekhaefer's Chryslers that won a total of 21 races and the championship in 1955.

Johnson won three of the next five races, beating Flock each time. Junior Johnson started 36 races and finished sixth in 1955 NASCAR championship points and money. But he raced little in 1956 and not at all in 1957 because of his incarceration. In 1958 he was back, returning to the top 10 with six wins and five more in 1959. He became known as a hard-charger, a "win-it-or-break-it" kind of driver.

But it was the 1960 Daytona 500 that made Junior Johnson's name famous. The first Daytona 500 took place in February 1959 on the newly constructed Daytona International Speedway, built by Bill France. Daytona Beach car builder Smokey Yunick and driver Paul Goldsmith left little doubt after the July 1959 Firecracker 250 at Daytona that Pontiac was the car to

beat on NASCAR's fastest track.

Ray Fox was a flinty New Hampshire mechanic who moved to the warm weather of Daytona Beach, where he operated a garage. Fox had established himself as one of the top mechanics of the NASCAR beach-racing era. Fox received a call just eight days before the 1960 Daytona 500 from John Masoni, owner of the Daytona Beach Kennel Club, who wanted to be represented in the race. Fox told him there wasn't enough time to build a car, but Masoni returned the following

Above: Darel Dieringer and Junior Johnson each won 1965 Daytona 500 qualifying races. Right: Fred Lorenzen was Johnson's closest rival throughout the 1965 NASCAR season.

Above: Johnson's "Yellow Banana" Ford was built in 1966 with the full knowledge of Bill France Sr. to show what it would take for a Ford to compete with Chrysler's Hemis. The car raced only once. Right: Cale Yarborough enjoyed his best seasons and won three NASCAR championships racing for Junior Johnson.

day and offered to pay double what Fox would otherwise charge to build a race car.

On the track, the car, a year-old 1959 Chevrolet with a "little" 348 engine, was bog slow compared with the more powerful Pontiacs. The story has been told many times how, giving away up to 30 mph to the Pontiacs, Johnson became discouraged and was ready to go home if Fox could find another driver.

Johnson told Higgins and Waid what he learned next. "Cotton Owens, in a Pontiac, came by and I got behind him. Right on his rear bumper. And I stayed right there! We came back to the garage and Cotton walked over to me. 'Boy, you've sure got that thing running,' Cotton said. What he didn't know was that I had discovered the aerodynamic draft at Daytona. I wanted to be sure what I'd hit on, so I went back out to practice alone. The car was still the same – pretty slow. So I came onto pit road and sat there waitin' for some Pontiacs to come by. I got in with them on the track. And I stayed up."

In the race, Johnson used a similar strategy as the Pontiacs fell one by one until only Goldsmith in the

black-and-gold Smokey Yunick Pontiac was on the lead lap, although Johnson had track position on Goldsmith. With 30 laps to go, a lapped car towed Goldsmith past Johnson, who stuck close to the Pontiac's rear bumper. Then, with just 10 laps remaining, "The back glass popped out of Bobby's car and flew into the air," Johnson told Higgins and Waid. "I think our speed and the circumstances combined to create a vacuum that sucked that back glass right out." Junior Johnson won the 1960 Daytona 500, and Bobby Johns finished second.

That race and other similar stories combined to give Junior Johnson a kind of Robin Hood appeal with his fans – David versus Detroit's Goliath.

Junior Johnson's legend continued to grow as Detroit flirted with NASCAR in the early 1960s. Factory support had helped NASCAR grow in the 1950s until a resolution by the Automobile Manufacturers Association in June 1957 suddenly swore off any future direct support. The resolution was drawn up under pressure from Congress for the automakers to focus on safety. But according to Greg Fielden, "Within a few

months, some or most of the factories were conducting racing business under the table." Under the table, that is, until Ford announced in 1962 that it would return to NASCAR giving its full support to the team of Holman-Moody and its star driver, Fred Lorenzen.

Lorenzen was the opposite of Junior Johnson. He was a northerner from the Chicago suburb of Elmhurst. He was a carpenter, with no connection to the land. He was blond, articulate, and he was also fast. He is still often referred to as NASCAR's first Golden Boy. Junior Johnson was the only driver who could race with Lorenzen's factory-backed Holman-Moody Ford in 1963, and he did it in a privately entered Chevrolet.

MYSTERY MOTORS AND THE YELLOW BANANA

General Motors continued to do its best to keep its brands out of auto racing. But it couldn't always keep the back door locked.

Three teams, including Fox, Yunick and 1960 NASCAR champion Rex White, each received a delivery of some very special Chevrolet engine parts in late 1962. These parts gave rise to the fabled 427 "Mystery Motors" in 1963. The parts the three teams received reportedly included special blocks, forged steel crankshafts and strengthened connecting rods. But it was the cylinder heads that gave the engines their unique character. The intake and exhaust valves were canted at different angles to increase combustion efficiency. This unusual feature also led to the heads being referred to as "porcupine heads." As much as 500 horsepower was claimed from the engines set up for stock car racing.

Johnson won the first of two 100-mile qualifying races in the Ray Fox Chevrolet at a speed of 164.083, more than three mph faster than Fireball Robert's pole-winning Ford. Rookie Johnny Rutherford won the second 100-mile race in Yunick's black-and-gold No. 13 Chevrolet at an even faster speed, 165.183. Only Rutherford was running at the finish, four laps down in ninth place, in a race that saw Fords sweep the first five positions, but the Mystery Motor was the story of the 1963 Daytona 500.

The rest of 1963 was a barnstorming season. Chevrolet versus Ford. Junior Johnson versus Freddy Lorenzen. Johnson led 21 of the 33 races he entered and won seven, while Lorenzen won six races and became the first NASCAR driver to win $100,000 in a single season. The crowds were on their feet all season long, and sports writers wrote that Ford spent $5 million trying to catch Junior Johnson.

Johnson started the 1964 season in a Dodge prepared by Ray Fox and ended the season in Banjo Matthews' Ford sponsored by Holly Farms, then a local poultry producer in Wilkes County. And, of course, Junior Johnson

Junior Johnson was known as a fierce competitor. Yet here, he helps change an engine in a rival Holman-Moody Ford.

met Tom Wolfe during the 1964 season. Something was bound to come of that. "That Wolfe guy was something else," Johnson later told Tom Higgins. "He showed up down here in Wilkes County talkin' funny and wearin' fancy clothes, including spats. Spats!"

The 1965 season, Johnson's last as a driver, was something else, too. His best ever, by most accounts. Driving the yellow No. 26 Holly Farms Ford, he beat Lorenzen's Ford on the last lap of their Daytona qualifying race. He won four out of five races in May. He won at North Wilkesboro, now paved, for the first time since 1958. He won on dirt. He won the Southern 500 at Darlington, on NASCAR's first super-speedway, and he won the Old Dominion 500 on Martinsville, Va.'s paper clip-shaped, one-half-mile track. He won 13 races in all in 1965, as well as 18 top-five finishes and 19 top 10s. In just 14 seasons, Junior Johnson started 313 NASCAR Grand National races, won 50 and sat on

the pole 46 times. And then he hung up his helmet and reinvented the role of NASCAR team owner.

But he wasn't quite finished behind the wheel. Six drivers were in and out of Johnson's No. 26 Ford during the 1966 season, including Junior himself. Bobby Issac started the season in the Holly Farms Ford before Junior released him to find a more competitive ride with a Dodge or Plymouth team. Curtis Turner started several races, Johnson drove eight races, and Indy car driver Gordon Johncock drove two races late in the season. But the race best remembered was the only time Fred Lorenzen drove for Junior Johnson, in a car that raced only once but has gone down in stock car history as the "Yellow Banana."

NASCAR's woes continued in 1966. Chrysler's Hemi was allowed to race again, and Ford responded with a boycott of its own. General Motors maintained its no-racing policy. Desperate to bring back fans, rules

Johnson's 1966 Holly Farms Ford team with crew chief Herb Nab laid the foundation for the success of Junior Johnson & Associates. Note above the casual environment compared with today's NASCAR pits.

INGLE HOLLOW

J unior Johnson's team raced out of a sprawling shop complex in Ingle Hollow near Ronda, N.C., an address that became famous worldwide. By all rights, the race shop should be designated as a National Historic Landmark.

It wasn't just a race shop. Junior Johnson & Associates became the top team in NASCAR and stayed on top for years. Junior and Flossie Johnson's home was built on the hillside overlooking the shop, and he raised 90,000 chickens in his hen houses

to sell to Holly Farms. Whenever NASCAR's top series raced at the nearby North Wilkesboro Speedway, anyone who was there to race was welcome at Ingle Hollow.

But they had to beat Junior Johnson to win. As a team owner, his cars won 139 races. In 15 years between 1972 and 1986, Johnson's teams won six NASCAR championships and were first or second 12 times. Cale Yarborough and Darrell Waltrip each won three championships with Junior Johnson teams in the best years of their careers. Dale Earnhardt was quoted by writer Marty Dutton as recalling a race where he was trying to stay in front of Cale Yarborough in Junior Johnson's No. 11: "I'm doing my best to stay in front of Cale, and he's beating my back bumper off. It's five

were bent. Bill France himself asked Johnson to build a car to show that a Ford could be competitive. Fred Lorenzen drove the car in the August Dixie 400 in Atlanta. Johnson's car was a full-size Ford Galaxie, but the many aerodynamic tweaks, the distinctively bowed

silhouette and the yellow Holly Farms paint gave the car its nickname. Lorenzen led 23 laps before a blown tire caused the car to crash out of the race.

After a first season like 1966, things could only get better. And, eventually, they did.

Above left: Darrell Waltrip and Junior Johnson, who also won three NASCAR championships together, enjoy a victory at North Wilkesboro in 1984. Above right: The partnership of Junior Johnson, Bill Elliott and crew chief Tim Brewer produced a victory in their very first race, the 1992 Gatorade 125 qualifying race at Daytona. Below: Junior Johnson and his No. 3 Chevrolet have been guests at the Goodwood Festival of Speed in England.

laps to go, three to go, and one to go and he's knocking me sideways. I won the race, then Junior walks up and says, 'Boy, you better be glad I wasn't in that race car.' I got scared he'd want to whip my butt."

Johnson also brought most of the best sponsors into NASCAR's modern era, which began with the Winston Cup schedule in 1972. Hell, Junior Johnson brought Winston to NASCAR. He first approached the R.J. Reynolds Tobacco Company, also a local company, to sponsor his team. "Seeing that they couldn't advertise on television anymore, I thought racing would be good for them. I think I was asking for $800,000 for my team. They came back to me and said they had $400 million for advertising, so I introduced them to NASCAR. I guess I sold myself out of a sponsorship, but I got plenty of that Winston money from the championships we won," Johnson told the author with a laugh.

Junior Johnson's teams usually enjoyed the best sponsors in NASCAR. In an era when STP, Purolator and Royal Crown Cola were considered good sponsorships, Junior Johnson's teams always had something a little better. Holly Farms gave way to First National City Travelers Checks, followed by Busch Beer, Mountain Dew and Pepsi, then a decade with Budweiser, as well as Amoco, Maxwell House and McDonald's.

And Junior Johnson made it look easy. Whether he was standing wordlessly with one foot on the pit wall during a long race or telling a sponsor what he needed from them, his cool expression was the same. He was Junior Johnson. Everybody wanted to be with Junior Johnson.

LAST DAYS

In 1992 Junior Johnson signed the most popular driver in NASCAR, Bill Elliott, to drive the No. 11 Budweiser Ford. It appeared to be the creation of a super-team. Johnson had won more championships than any other owner in NASCAR history. Elliott and his family-owned team in Dawsonville, Ga., had almost single-handedly brought Ford back into NASCAR in the mid-1980s, winning the 1985 and 1987 Daytona 500s and the 1988 championship, and returning legions of Ford fans to NASCAR. Elliott was also the first driver to win a $1 million bonus offered by Winston in 1985, earning the nicknames "Awesome Bill from Dawsonville" and "Million Dollar Bill." He became the first NASCAR driver to appear on the cover of *Sports Illustrated*..

By 1992, Johnson and Elliott were both at a crossroads. While many drivers enjoyed the best years of their careers in Johnson's No. 11, the Budweiser-sponsored team hadn't won a championship in six seasons. Meanwhile, Elliott had grown weary of the demands of both running the race team with his brothers Ernie and Dan and racing.

Amoco came on board as a major sponsor of No. 11, and Johnson also entered a second car for Sterling Marlin, sponsored by General Foods' Maxwell House

Left: Junior Johnson's Dew Crew was the best-prepared team in NASCAR in 1981. It was Darrell Waltrip's first season with the team, an opportunity he called "a dream come true." The team won the NASCAR championship, Waltrip's first.

coffee. The new team immediately qualified 1-2 for the 1992 Daytona 500 and appeared to be the cars to beat in the race. But after a brief rain delay and a restart after lap 80, Ernie Irvan took out both Johnson cars while leading in a crash that included 15 cars.

Elliott came back to win the next four races in a row at Rockingham, Richmond, Atlanta and Darlington. It looked as if he was going to win everything. But by the final race of the season, back at Atlanta, five teams had a chance to win the championship, including Elliott, Davey Allison and Alan Kulwicki. Elliott won the race and, it seemed, the championship. But as the team and sponsors ran from their pit to Victory Lane, a radio call indicated that something was wrong. Kulwicki had led the most laps in the race – by one. A miscalcula-

tion in Elliott's pit gave Kulwicki, not Elliott, the 1992 NASCAR Winston Cup championship.

Johnson's team was packed with big egos and the success to back up their swagger. But after the Atlanta race, the air seemed to go out of the team. Crew chief Tim Brewer, who had worked with Johnson for 15 years, was gone over the winter. Johnson and Elliott appeared to be uneasy with one another, even at sponsor appearances. This continued through the 1993 and 1994 seasons, while Johnson replaced Maxwell House with McDonald's on his second car. The sponsorship was McDonald's first entry into NASCAR racing and was coveted by teams including Richard Petty and Joe Gibbs. But it was Junior Johnson who brought McDonald's into NASCAR. Sterling Marlin was gone from the team, and Hut Stricklin was placed in the seat of the McDonald's Ford, and then was replaced by hard-charging Jimmy Spencer the following year.

At the end of his three-year contract in 1994, Elliott announced that he was rejoining his brothers Ernie and Dan Elliott to form Bill Elliott Racing in the family's Dawsonville shop. He openly courted McDonald's and Amoco for the sponsorship. McDonald's went with Elliott, while Amoco offered to split its sponsorship between both teams. Elliott accepted, and Johnson refused. It wasn't his way of doing things.

Instead, Johnson signed Lowe's Home Improvement to its first NASCAR sponsorship. Lowe's was another local company, based in North Wilkesboro. It was a model sponsorship in which major suppliers to the retailer contributed to the cost of the sponsorship and benefited from promotion and advertising. The driver was Brett Bodine, one of three Bodine brothers racing in NASCAR. But, while the team qualified for every race, they showed only two top-10 finishes for the season.

At the end of the 1995 season, Junior Johnson sold the team to Bodine and walked away from NASCAR after 43 years. The growing team of Rick Hendrick, which already included 1995 Winston Cup champion Jeff Gordon with Dupont sponsorship, former champion Terry Labonte with Kellogg's, and Ken Shrader with Budweiser, won the Lowe's sponsorship.

Above: Elliott's 1992 Budweiser team won five races including the final race of the season at Atlanta, but Alan Kulwicki won the championship.

Junior Johnson campaigned actively for presidential candidate Barak Obama in 2008, including this appearance with Hillary Clinton at the North Carolina Auto Racing Hall of Fame following Obama's nomination.

REDEMPTION

Johnson refused to go to the tracks where he wasn't involved any longer. Junior and Flossie were childless and divorced in 1995. Johnson married Lisa Suzanne, and together the couple had two children, Robert and Meredith. Johnson doted on his new family. He built a 14,000-square-foot house for them, not far from Ingle Hollow. He added to his large herd of Santa Gertrudis cattle, and a flock of guinea hens watches over the property and signals intruders. He also built an elaborate swimming pool and a large pool deck behind the house. It was more than anyone had ever had in Wilkes County.

He also put up a barn where he manages the 200-acre farm and meets with his hired men every morning. In the corner of the barn are a stove and a long table where Johnson serves up breakfast most mornings.

His exile ended in 1998 with the 50th Anniversary of NASCAR. The celebration of the fastest-growing sport in America couldn't turn its back on Junior Johnson. He was honored throughout the 50th anniversary season and enjoyed himself. He started taking his young son to race tracks. He was invited by Lord March to attend the Goodwood Festival of Speed in England and race his white No. 3 Chevrolet up the Goodwood estate's long driveway. When the 50th anniversary of the Daytona 500 followed in 2008, it was Junior Johnson who drove the pace car.

Using his name, he helped start new businesses that created jobs in Wilkes County. In 2008 he stumped for presidential candidate Barack Obama, making appearances on occasion with Hillary Clinton. But his latest venture is the danged'est thing anyone ever could have imagined.

In 1986, Junior Johnson received a Presidential Pardon from Ronald Reagan for his 1956 moonshining conviction. A section of North Carolina Highway 421, where Junior Johnson once hauled moonshine, was named the Junior Johnson Highway by the state in 2004. Then, in 2007, Junior Johnson introduced his own brand of whiskey, legally. Junior Johnson's Midnight Moon is produced in North Carolina's last legal distillery. He frequently makes appearances at race tracks and liquor stores to promote the product, which is triple distilled and, he says, "smoother than vodka and better than whiskey."

"Listen at him – there he goes!" wrote Wolfe. Junior Johnson. Again. AQ

ART TECH

Steve Maloney's West Coast

The Gilmore Brothers Department Store in Kalamazoo, Mich., is as likely a starting point for a gifted artist as the home of a merchant on Pokrovskaya Street in Liozno, Belarus, the ancestral home of modernist master Marc Chagall, Steve Maloney's inspirational muse. The creations of both are richly colored abstract visions from the rational, pragmatic DNA of a businessman's son. Chagall went off to the cafes and soirees of Paris; Maloney went off to the American School in Lugano, Switzerland. Each went for the opportunity to experience the rich creativity of European culture.

Typical of Steve Maloney's sense of humor and unique flare, "Carumba," seen above.

BY LARRY CRANE

Maloney's work on display at the Petro Museum.

aloney returned to his hometown to begin a career in the family business. The more he understood the creative requirements of the environment, the more challenged he became. His fine-menswear shop soon included early importations of Abercrombie & Fitch and a new line of haberdashery from a young New York designer named Ralph Lauren. But the business was moving too slowly for Maloney. An investment in a thriving machine-tool manufacturing company reignited the creative gene. The company product lines prospered from Maloney's artful eye. Soon, he was able to be part of an old friend's car hobby, to the extent that they built off-road racing machines to their own designs and entered the early Baja 1000 events.

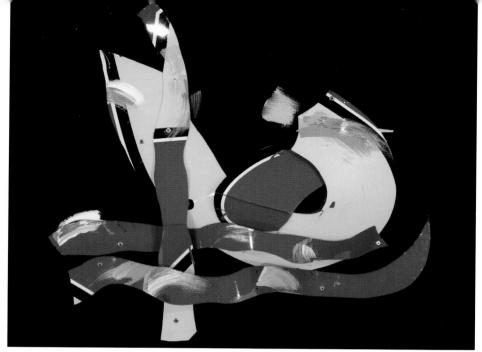

Above: One of Maloney's Boogie Woogie variations, "Car 25."

The two recorded two actual finishes, testament to their skills, courage and Wild West-like spirit.

"I have always been interested in and impressed by velocity and the mobile spirit of America," Maloney said. "Born and raised in the Midwest, I was drawn as much to the countryside as to the broad-shouldered cityscapes, checkered cabs, airplanes, auto racing and the colorful cultures and images that surround them – these [latter] are the mechanisms that fire my imagination."

Further establishing Maloney's automotive genetic makeup, after leaving the retail business, his grandfather purchased a farm with several barns on a bucolic piece of land northwest of Kalamazoo. That farm now contains the senior Maloney's large collection of American and European classic cars; it also includes several others from Classic Car Club of America members and goes by the name of The Gilmore Classic Car Club of America Museum.

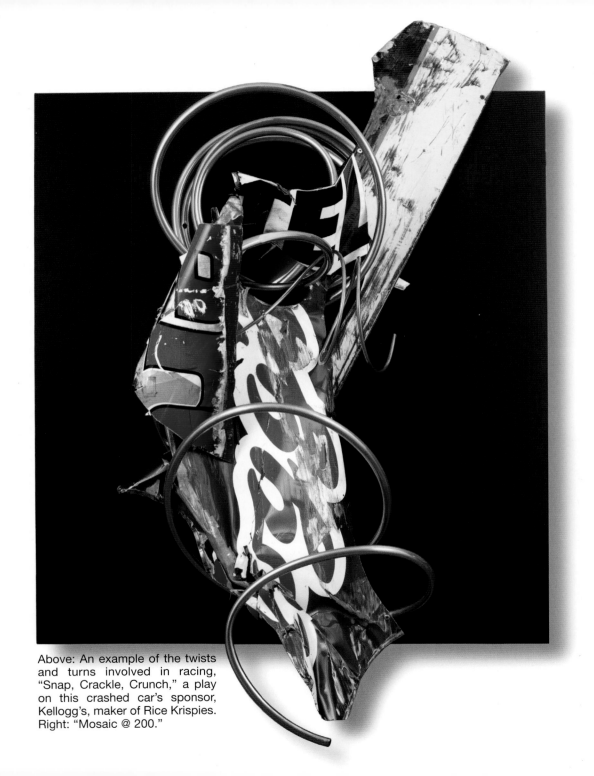

Following much of the family's incremental migration west, California became Maloney's new home; its diverse culture and topography became his new inspiration. He derives his automotive pleasures from a '47 Ford Woodie, a '66 Mustang and an Aston Martin DB9.

"Since moving to Rancho Santa Fe, Calif., a charming village I've called home since 1993," Maloney said, "I have witnessed the progress of Southern California's diverse populations, the transformation of its small towns, and the installation of the air hubs and intricate strands of asphalt that connect them to the world beyond. And I have been inspired by it all."

In 2002, Maloney and his wife Yvonne founded the Maloney Gallery in Rancho Santa Fe's historic La Flecha building. The vast space is filled with the different visions of their prolific partnership.

"With conspicuous colors, textured surfaces, authentic materials and humor, my work has been enthusias-

Above: An example of the twists and turns involved in racing, "Snap, Crackle, Crunch," a play on this crashed car's sponsor, Kellogg's, maker of Rice Krispies. Right: "Mosaic @ 200."

tically received and favorably reviewed in a number of exhibitions," Maloney notes. "My aim is to create art that celebrates America's realities in an accessible and approachable way. For instance, I fashioned the Vrooom series of visually exciting sculptural works

Humor in art: "Speedy Lap Dog."

A second studio is now open in Palm Springs, Calif., and visitors are welcomed by appointment to either studio. The Maloney Gallery at 16904 Via de Santa Fe, Rancho Santa Fe, is open Monday to Friday from 10 a.m. to 5 p.m.

ONE PERSON'S TRASH ...

As part of Maloney's *This is Where the Rubber Meets the Road* series, Maloney lent sophistication to NASCAR's biggest event when he created original works at a trackside studio during the 50th running of the Daytona 500 in 2008. Set beneath palm trees on a patch of green, mere steps from Pit Road and the Daytona 500 Club, Maloney's tented studio was the scene of blistering creativity as he fashioned sculptural pieces from bodywork and components of Daytona Prototype and Grand Touring race cars collected during that season's Rolex 24 at Daytona, combined with other NASCAR sheet metal.

Along with his trackside studio, Maloney exhibited his *This is Where the Rubber Meets the Road* series of 31 mixed-media works created from dinged, dented and shredded parts of actual NASCAR race cars. The exhibition was on display at the Daytona 500 Club through April 1, 2008.

"Steve's unique work is something that every NASCAR fan should see," Daytona International Speedway President Robin Braig told the press. "The trackside studio opened up a new perspective on the sport of auto racing to fans and art lovers alike, and we enjoyed seeing Steve in action throughout our historic weekend."

The crashed-sheet-metal series also appeared at the CODA Gallery in the Soho district of Manhattan. The exhibition ran in late 2007, concurrent with the 2007 NASCAR NEXTEL Cup Series Champions Week. One New York newspaper stated Maloney's approach well: "The wall-mounted and board-backed 'contemporary sculptural collages as well as freestanding sculptures' reveal the artist's innovative take on color and form, with dented sheet metal, tire scraps

out of well-designed motorcycle parts for the 100th anniversary of Harley-Davidson in 2003."

Maloney's Speed Blur series of abstract oil paintings from 2003 is specifically suited for the elegant confines of private jets, while the Broadway series of postmodern paintings from 2000 "invokes mass-media images to frame the audacity of New York's most vital thoroughfare. In 2003, I transformed tons of commonplace

items that had been confiscated at Californian airport security checkpoints in the wake of 9/11 into Banned Booty, a mixed-media series that reveals the effects of the attack on everyday American life."

That series is now in the permanent collection of the Museum of Flight in Seattle. It recently traveled to the Kansas Cosmosphere & Space Center, where it was exhibited for three months.

Above: "Boogie Woogie." Right: "Tower of Speed.

and scuffed advertising logos merg[ing] into dizzying arrays of previously mechanized beauty. While casual observers may need to rubberneck before realizing where the materials in works like *Boogie Woogie No. 4, Homage To Mondrian* came from, NASCAR fans will know in an instant."

Maloney's response: "You don't have to be an art history major to understand *This is Where the Rubber Meets the Road.* To me, NASCAR is much more Americana then Andy Warhol's soup cans."

Above: "Broadway Barbie." Below: "Gentlemen Start Your Engines." Below left: Maloney with "Winding Road" at the 2008 Pebble Beach Concours d'Elegance.

Motordom's Mandrake
Giorgetto Giugiaro

Towering over all other auto designers in the 21st century is the tall figure of Giorgetto Giugiaro, a prolific designer of automobiles who doesn't particularly like cars. He's the accidental master of his chosen field.

BY KARL LUDVIGSEN
COLOR PHOTOGRAPHY BY WINSTON GOODFELLOW

For the historic 50th Turin Salon in early November 1968, Italy's coachbuilders were out in full force. Vignale had the latest Maserati Indy, a rebodied Matra and a Ferrari "station wagon" commissioned by Luigi Chinetti. Bertone showed the Alfa-based Carabo that was the season's star so far, while Ghia wheeled out three studies on Maserati and Serenissima chassis. Pininfarina exerted a full-court press with seven cars, all in a "pearl or hand-cream white," including a Ferrari P6 study and a wedge-styled Alfa Romeo Type 33 roadster.

Could any newcomer prevail against competition like this? Surprisingly, one did. On the Bizzarrini stand was a Chevy-powered midengined machine called "Manta" in a striking form. A rebodied racing car, it shocked and amazed with its one-box design fronted by a windscreen sloped at 15 degrees from the horizontal. Its driver sat centrally with a passenger on each side. "It really looked like a projectile," said Giotto Bizzarrini, who provided its chassis.

The outrageous, yet handsome, Manta marked the official debut of Giorgetto Giugiaro and his new Ital Design company. If it was his aim to stake out a prominent position as a designer to be reckoned with, the 28-year-old succeeded in spades. "The strongest rival to Pininfarina and Bertone for the Carrozzeria sweepstakes," said *Road & Track*, "was undoubtedly the Bizzarrini Manta." The influential magazine put the Manta on its March 1969 cover, fronting a major Griff Borgeson feature on Giugiaro that declared "as an individual he dominates his art as perhaps no one has before."

Was this impressive newcomer a one-car wonder? Giugiaro swiftly proved that he had more strings to his bow. On the Alfa 33 chassis in 1969, he showed his Iguana coupe with scaly features that inspired its name. A major tour de force in 1970 was his Tapiro on Porsche's 914/6 platform, a masterly wedge-shaped exercise with transparent gull-wing access to both cockpit and engine compartment. A production car in 1971 with all the glamour of a concept car was Giugiaro's 1971 Bora, the first midengined Maserati for the road.

Giugiaro's stop-in-your-tracks designs correlated with his persona early on. Here, the Chevy-powered Manta marked the young designers official debut on the world stage

the famous names of *carrozzerie* who were happy to use his designs without giving him credit.

As the foregoing encomiums suggest, Giugiaro is a man who brings a pure aesthetic professionalism to car design. Not for him the "gasoline-in-the-blood" philosophy of which Detroit has long been enamored. "I would have liked to have been an artist," he said, "instead of which I am a sculptor of cars. Working on cars was not a choice but something that happened."

AN ARTIST AT HEART

Giorgetto was born on Aug. 7, 1938, as one of three children of Mario and Maria Giugiaro. His was the third generation of a family of painters who specialized in large-scale frescos in churches, palazzos and public buildings. His birthplace was the town of Garessio, with a population of 6,000, some 60 miles southwest of Turin in the Maritime Alps near the coast. At the age of 12, he began studying

Giugiaro's 1972 Maserati Boomerang (above) came a decade after his design on this 1962 Ferrari, right.

An ultimate expression of Giorgetto Giugiaro's inventiveness was his Maserati Boomerang of 1972. Sloped at an excruciating 13 degrees from horizontal, its windscreen was, said one commentator, "bordering on the very limits of feasibility." Built on a midengined chassis, the Boomerang took viewers to "the world of unbridled fantasy where Giugiaro treats us to a treasury of his visual ideas. The entire composition thrives on trapezoids and alternating dihedrals." Almost as extreme was Giugiaro's 1972 design for the Lotus Esprit, which ultimately reached production.

With this stunning series of spectacular sports and concept cars, Giugiaro and his Ital Design earned a prominent place among the Italian coachbuilders whose imaginative and influential designs were the envy of the world. For those in the know, however, since the beginning of the 1960s, Giorgetto Giugiaro had been a man to reckon with as designer and innovator. His precocity had been hidden, however, behind

One of the first, if not the first, official designs in the Giugiaro canon is stated to be the British Gordon GT, which came to market as the plastic-bodied, Chevy-powered Gordon-Keeble. His profile drawing of it is dated Dec. 31, 1959.

painting at Turin's Accademia di Belle Arti. Under multitalented Professor Eugenio Colmo, he added illustration and fashion design to his artistic portfolio.

Nicknamed "Golia" or "Goliath," the protean Colmo made no small impression on the young Giugiaro: "He was really a 'maestro,' an artist who was so deeply convinced I could become a good artist that he persuaded my parents to let me leave home to enter his school of fine arts. I remember enjoying the design of all sorts of items for hours every day. But I learned more than just fine arts: he taught us how to live and how to think about broad aspects of life. He was also a sort of philosopher, as an artist needs to be.

"I wanted to be a painter and so did my family," Giugiaro continued, "who encouraged me to study and paint." But practicality entered

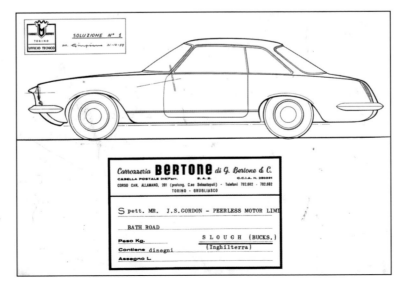

the picture. "One day my professor said to me: being an artist is hard, you starve. Use your talent for drawing in other disciplines." The opportunity to do just that arose when Giugiaro found himself short of funds to continue his education.

In 1955, an exhibition of academic work included some of the student's satirical caricatures of automobiles. A nephew of Giugiaro's professor was Dante Giacosa, nearing the end of a great career as Fiat's chief engineer. Seeing the drawings at the professor's suggestion, Giacosa divined potential and recommended the young man to Fiat's advanced-design group, which made him an offer. "I decided to take the job at Fiat to have a steady salary," said Giugiaro. He'd just turned 17 when he joined Fiat in September of 1955.

"There I discovered the world of creativ-

promising, said the acknowledged master. "Please do something more concrete," he asked. At the end of the Salon, Giugiaro returned with two fully worked-out versions of his idea. "Both met with suspicion," related D.O. Cozzi. "Bertone refused to believe that Giugiaro alone had done the work. [Giugiaro] was angered and offended and, typically, he asked for an assignment. After two weekends in the Bertone studios he presented his first complete car: the Alfa 2600 coupe."

Not slow to recognize talent, Bertone offered the young man a job. He had a vacancy, Franco Scaglione having left to set up on his own. "In the beginning," Giugiaro said, "there were just the two of us in the design office: Bertone and I." In fact, the first official design in the Giugiaro canon is stated to be the British Gordon GT, which came to market as the plastic-bodied, Chevy-powered Gordon-Keeble. His profile drawing of it is dated Dec. 31, 1959. However, its lines

The master at work: sketching the Panda (above) and with the custom Mustang ordered by Automobile Quarterly's L. Scott Bailey in 1964 (below, Nuccio Bertone on left).

ity," Giorgetto Giugiaro said of his stay at Fiat, where the imaginative and experienced Luigi Fabio Rapi was in charge of special-vehicle design. "But I still dreamed about becoming a painter," Giugiaro admitted. The Fiat job was just a way for him to earn the funds he needed to continue his education. At the Mirafiori headquarters, he gained the skills of vehicle rendering and presentation while polishing his technical drawing ability.

Tall and well-built, young Giugiaro was a keen skier and winner of several amateur competitions. Looking forward to the 1959 winter season, he had his eye on a new pair of skis but lacked the discretionary funds. He conceived the idea of moonlighting for a coachbuilder by selling a design he had in mind. Through a friend, he was introduced to Nuccio Bertone at 1959's Turin Salon. "For me, he was a creative Olympian," Giugiaro recalled, "a superhuman being, and I approached him with great timidity and circumspection."

Assessing the well-presented young man on his stand during the show's press day, Bertone asked him to sketch what he had in mind. His design looked

were close kin to those of the Alfa Romeo 2000/2600 Sprint, first shown at Turin late in 1960.

The Bertone years were crucial in the evolution of the young designer. "If I had not known Mr. Bertone – without the experience and type of opportunity I had at his firm – I would never have become the car designer I am today," Giugiaro told Giancarlo Perini in 1974. "He understood me and gave me the confidence and freedom which enabled me to design cars. I hope I gave his company many good designs in return."

Giugiaro's Bertone period was notable for a project dear to the heart of *Automobile Quarterly*. This was the commissioning of Bertone by editor and publisher L. Scott Bailey to rebody the latest American sensation, the Ford Mustang. A meeting between Bailey and Bertone in the autumn of 1964 resulted in the decision to produce the one-off design that was premiered in April of 1965 at the New York International Automobile Show. Striking in a light metallic tur-

Another stand-out design for Maserati, the Bora. Below, Giugiaro in his office, 1985.

quoise, superbly finished inside and out, the AQ Mustang carried this magazine's Quatrefoil as well as the Bertone badge on its flanks.

The Bertone-bodied Mustang and its gestation were introduced in Volume 4, Number 2, of *Automobile Quarterly*. In editor Bailey's article, a photo showed

Nuccio Bertone "and his young designer-in-charge Giugiaro" assessing the wood model to which the body panels were shaped. Inasmuch as it was not the practice of Bertone or indeed other Italian coachbuilders to identify their collaborators, even to specialist publications, this may well have been the debut appearance in print of Giorgetto Giugiaro in his chosen profession of automobile designer.

creation. "When I entered the field of cars, there was already a form, a discussion, a language about cars," he told the author in 1974. "A car had two parts: one part was the side view and the other part was the plan view. In the Testudo, I broke down these two parts. This was my first attempt to avoid having two separate parts but rather to have one part blending into the other.

"I wanted to express to myself that I was able to do

The De Tomaso Mangusta was one of Giugiaro's most endearing designs.

A pivotal concept car for both Bertone and Giugiaro was the Corvair Testudo, for "tortoise," introduced at Geneva in 1963. Created at a time when GM's Styling Staff under Bill Mitchell had friendly relations with Turin's coachbuilders, the Testudo was based on a Corvair chassis that GM had provided, much as it had also done with Pininfarina. Unlike the latter's elegant but sober designs, Giugiaro's creation was an ultralow coupe with a sleek, carapace-like body and a canopy-cum-doors that hinged up and forward. Nuccio Bertone personally drove it from Turin to Geneva for the Salon.

For Giorgetto Giugiaro, the Testudo was a landmark

something, that I was able to give something of myself, from my mind alone," Giugiaro added, "that I was no longer following a chain, following other ideas. With the Testudo, I proved to myself that I was able to break with the past and begin with something coming from my own imagination. I believe it was a radically new kind of car, a new concept. In my opinion, it seemed to provide a new source for car designs. That was a car with which I really felt I contributed to car designing."

The creation of the Testudo was one of the miracles of speed so characteristic of the Turin *carrozzerie*. "I started working on the Testudo on the third of

January," Giugiaro said, "and on the third of March, the car was driven from Turin to Geneva for the show." If the Testudo – called "dynamic but awkward" by *Road & Track* – made its impact by dramatic exaggeration, another Giugiaro concept car of this era had an appeal that was more subtle but no less profound. This was the Alfa Romeo Giulia 1600 Canguro, built on the TZ's tubular space frame. Although looking nothing like a kangaroo, said Griff Borgeson, "it appears to be on the verge of catapulting forward even in repose, hence the name."

Above: 1968 Maserati Ghibli coupé 2+2. Below: 1972 Maserati Ghibli spider.

Conceived as a more attractive and wind-cheating body for Alfa's Giulia Tubolare TZ, yet also offering interior habitability, the Canguro was sublimely, subtly curved and proportioned in a manner that rejected "top-view" and "side-view" conventions. Never realized in production by Alfa, one of its deeply regretted lost opportunities, the Canguro remains a touchstone of excellence for enthusiasts of the four-leaf clover, which was artfully incorporated in its vents behind the side windows.

In cover stories for *Road & Track* of June 1965, Griff Borgeson profiled both the Canguro and Nuccio Bertone – "Master of the Italian Style" – over 11 adulatory pages. Not once does the name "Giugiaro" appear, this almost five years into a career at Bertone that had substantially enhanced the coachbuilder's reputation and resulted in royalty-spinning production designs for Alfa Romeo, BMW, ASA, Simca, Iso, Fiat and Mazda. "Bertone had clearly gotten his money's worth," wrote D.O. Cozzi, "but not enough was passed on to Giugiaro for Giugiaro's liking." Also, the lack of credit for his work was beginning to gall.

By now industry insiders were well aware of the talent that lay behind Bertone's creations. An attractive offer was made by Ford's Cologne operation. "Ford offered me the best salary," said Giugiaro, "but I would have had to move to Germany. I preferred to stay in Turin and build cars as we have the best of everything here." Turin was also closer to the skiing the designer enjoyed.

Giugiaro joined Turin's Carrozzeria Ghia instead. This seemed promising but soon after his arrival in November of 1965, the company was bought by American interests that put émigré Argentinean Alejandro de Tomaso in charge. The most important results of the new alliance were visible at the 1966 Turin Salon in a magnificent new sports Maserati, the Ghibli, and an impressive midengined de Tomaso, the backbone-chassis Mangusta.

The schism with Bertone was creatively traumatic, said Giorgetto Giugiaro: "When I left Bertone, I was obliged to leave behind everything that I had contributed. All the shapes I had created at Bertone had to be left behind." This demanded of him a huge intel-

Giugiaro in the 1980s, content at work both in his office and at the drawing board.

lectual investment in a new design language. Though sublimely spectacular and destined to be one of the most-admired Maseratis, the Ghibli was the more conventional of the two.

"The Ghibli was made for a customer," said the designer, "and I wasn't sure that Maserati could understand what I wanted to say with its design, so I was obliged to change it slightly – but not too much."

the Ford-powered Mangusta made headlines. Using a design he'd originally conceived for a Bizzarrini chassis, Giugiaro created a hunched-down, sleek-lined bullet of a car that bespoke its substantial power. An audacious gull-wing design for its rear deck was breathtaking. Its interior was little more than a sketch, a flat dash with gauges, but its exterior was sublime. By dipping its door line and sloping its screen, the Mangusta

Nevertheless, when he left Ghia he again had regrets over what he'd had to leave behind: "When I did the Maserati Ghibli, it cost me a lot to leave that idea. The habit of being forced to abandon a design that you like forces you to give up being a romantic."

In contrast to the Ghibli, said Giugiaro, "I did the Mangusta for myself, as a way of expressing my ideas." At a time when midengined sports cars for the road were much in the news,

showed Giugiaro's first effort to guide the eye up and over the shape instead of along the belt line.

When quizzed early in his career about his favorite designs, Giorgetto Giugiaro never failed to mention the Ghibli and Mangusta. "There simply is no 'best' car," he said. "Many of them are good with respect to their functions. But several I am quite fond of are the Ghibli and the Mangusta." The effort needed to evolve a new design language for them had left its mark.

During his brief but turbulent and productive sojourn at Ghia, Giorgetto Giugiaro began to consider his future. "At Ghia, I could work quietly without trouble," he related. "But I wasn't working the whole day for Ghia. So I could look around and find other work. I started a separate activity, a business, together with two other persons. One had great knowledge of all technical matters and creation of engineering drawings [Aldo Mantovani] while the other knew methods and infrastructure [Luciano Bosio]. My aim was to create not only design ideas for someone else to realize but also everything that would be necessary to realize that idea."

Giugiaro and his partners in Ital Design rejected the traditional concept of a *carrozzeria* in the style of Pininfarina and Bertone, who were not only designing cars but also producing them. "I felt that the idea of a normal *carrozzeria* was already old," he told the author.

"I wanted to bring something new. The meaning of a *carrozzeria* is to become an industry and produce cars, but I didn't want to produce cars. I wanted to produce ideas. My concept is to leave production to the big industries." His company's main brush with manufacturing came when it helped BMW get its M1, a Giugiaro design, into production at Baur when Lamborghini was unable to build it. A few concept cars such as the 1991 Nazca and 1993 Aztec Barchetta have been built in small numbers.

The understanding of manufacturing of Giugiaro and his Ital Design partners was comprehensively tested from mid-1967, when they were commissioned by Alfa Romeo to take care of body design and engineering for an all-new car to be built in an all-new factory at Pomigliano d'Arco, near Naples. This was the birth of the Alfasud, which came to market at 1971's Turin Salon.

Both the car and its factory were the creation of a peripatetic Viennese engineer, Rudolf Hruska. He was the author of the Alfasud's flat-four water-cooled engine driving the front wheels and its coil-sprung suspension. Giugiaro first met Hruska in 1960 when the engineer, based in Milan but working in Turin, was assisting Bertone in the design of a pretty coupe body for Simca's 1000 model that came to market in 1962. Then they collaborated on the shape of the 1965 Fiat 850 Spider, a hugely successful model with 140,000 produced, and the 1967 Fiat Dino coupe.

Financially vital to newly formed Ital Design, the commission promised a chance to innovate. However, the job turned out to be a mixed blessing for Giugiaro, who found that "Alfa Romeo doesn't mind ruining the shape of a car to get the kind of aerodynamics they want. Perhaps when I design a car, people see it and say how bad it is, but they don't know that I was obliged to do it that

A product designed during his time at Volkswagen, the first Golf retained Giugiaro's design from presentation to production.

way for technical reasons and the most important one – aerodynamics."

A man of experience and determination who had helped plan the Volkswagen factory before the war, Rudy Hruska was a tough taskmaster. "It is really difficult to design a good-looking car while working with him," Giugiaro found. "The Alfasud could have been better styled but he wanted me to modify it here and there to get better aerodynamics and performance. We argued over every millimeter of difference!" One such argument was over trunk space, Hruska having presented the designer with a set of mandatory suitcases. To get them in while keeping to Hruska's desired shape required exposed hinges for the trunk lid – not the designer's preference!

"I never succeeded in persuading him to accept some of my proposals which contrasted with some of his ideas," Giugiaro said of Hruska. Nevertheless, he had great respect for the Austrian. "He gave me the technical understanding and feeling for the car, such things as practicality and functions," the designer explained in 1974. "Hruska is one of the best product engineers I have ever met."

His and the Ital Design team's work with Rudy Hruska and Alfa Romeo was vital to the next major step in the motor industry by Giorgetto Giugiaro. It came about in an interesting way, said the designer: "Kurt Lotz, who was president of the Volkswagen Group, came to the Turin Show in 1969. He walked around studying all the cars and taking note of the ones he liked best. Then he asked an important specialist journalist there to tell him about the designers of those cars. All the cars Mr. Lotz appreciated happened to be my designs. After answering his questions, the journalist introduced me to Mr. Lotz. A few weeks later, I started working for Volkswagen."

At first the opportunities in Wolfsburg seemed limited. Under Lotz, the Beetle's designated successor was a midengined small car being developed and styled by the Porsche office in Stuttgart. However, this was peremptorily terminated by Rudolf Leiding, who took over from Lotz in 1971. The experienced Leiding launched work instead on a completely new generation of cars. Giugiaro would be their stylist.

The designer looked back on this period as one of exceptional accomplishment. "I worked very well to my complete satisfaction with VW," he said, "even if the schedule was very short. Normally doing a new car takes three years, and I had to do this in three months! The Volkswagen Golf, Passat, Scirocco – all three."

When Assessing this episode, Giorgetto Giugiaro was of two minds. On the one hand, he said that "I regret that I hadn't enough time to develop these cars." On the other hand, he relished the purity of design that resulted from the need to create and tool them so quickly. He wasn't happy that VW insisted on round headlights for the Golf instead of the rectangular ones he wanted, though in fact they added interest to its

Above: Maserati Buran. Below: Putting wheels on the "tall boy" design concept for the 1978 Turin Salon, the Lancia Megagamma.

"face." He prevailed with rectangular lights in one of the Scirocco's versions.

On the Golf, Giugiaro employed a technique he first essayed on his Mangusta. He eliminated the traditional beltline, the upper surface of the car's main body along which the eye tends to travel. By doing this he aimed to have the eye moving in a different manner: "I tried to have the eye following the shape up over the windscreen instead of being broken as it had to travel back along the beltline." In this, the Golf's down-sloping hood and stiff screen cooperated.

When asked which of his designs entered production much as he presented them, Giorgetto Giugiaro credited "the first VW Golf and Scirocco, as well the Audi 80, the Fiat Panda, Uno, Punto and Grande Punto, the Lancia Delta, the Alfa Brera and 159 and the Lexus GS300." Perhaps not thinking it important enough, he didn't mention the Yugo Florida, which at its introduction in 1987 he considered a notably successful realization of his design.

These jobs and later projects called for expansion for Ital Design. Initially in Turin offices, the company moved in April of 1974 to bespoke premises in the city's Moncalieri district. There it continued the long series of design successes that have added luster to its name. At the beginning of 2007, Giugiaro and his son Fabrizio acquired all the outstanding shares in Ital Design, making it entirely a family property.

A project of which Giorgetto Giugiaro is especially proud is the starkly utilitarian Fiat Panda, introduced in 1980. Its presentation to Fiat left no questions unanswered with two full-size exterior models and one interior, four different side treatments and a study comparing the proposal with its rivals. Once approved,

Ital Design started production studies, built a master model, designed tooling, and within a year had built 20 rolling chassis and preproduction prototypes. Its four-wheel-drive version had a powerrain invented and patented by Ital Design.

Never hesitating to present solutions he sees as best for the automobile, Giugiaro has broken with the consensus on many occasions. "Going against the commonly held belief that low, wide and long is best for today's cars," he said, "with the Lancia Megagamma at the 1978 Turin Salon, I introduced the 'tall boy' concept and urged acceptance of it." This was a "tall car" that appeared four years before the similar Nissan Prairie, five ahead of the Chrysler Voyager and six years in advance of the Renault Espace.

"When I presented this vehicle to Fiat's Umberto Agnelli," Giugiaro recalled, "he said, 'Nice car. All that's required is the courage to produce it.' Unfortunately, the courage was lacking and, in my opinion, a great opportunity was missed, that of launching the modern trend for the MPV with a product marked 'Made in Italy.'" The

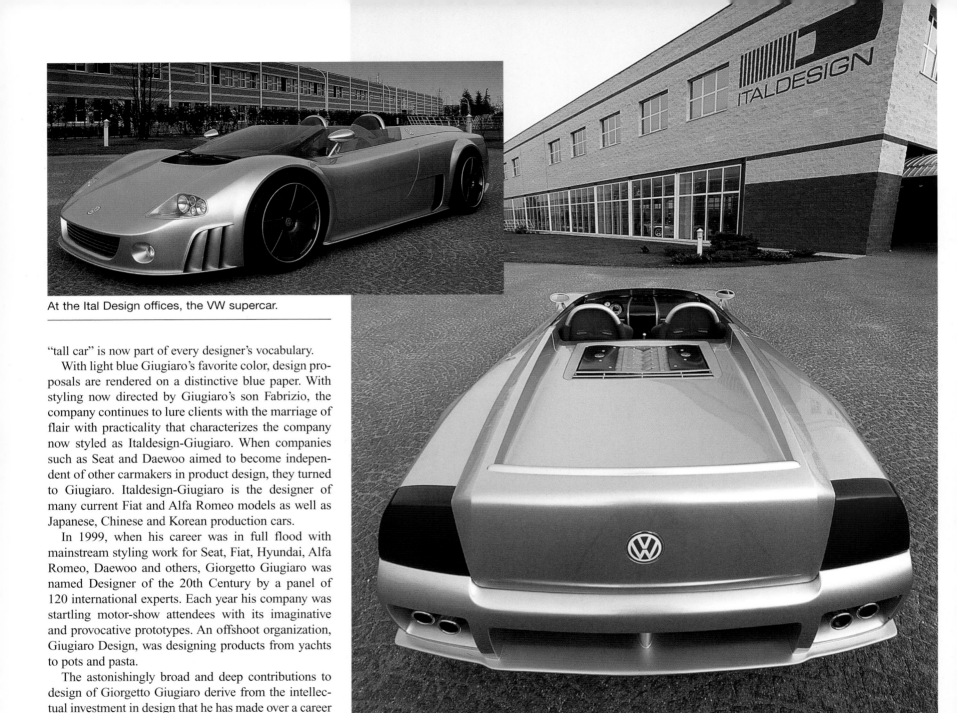

At the Ital Design offices, the VW supercar.

"tall car" is now part of every designer's vocabulary.

With light blue Giugiaro's favorite color, design proposals are rendered on a distinctive blue paper. With styling now directed by Giugiaro's son Fabrizio, the company continues to lure clients with the marriage of flair with practicality that characterizes the company now styled as Italdesign-Giugiaro. When companies such as Seat and Daewoo aimed to become independent of other carmakers in product design, they turned to Giugiaro. Italdesign-Giugiaro is the designer of many current Fiat and Alfa Romeo models as well as Japanese, Chinese and Korean production cars.

In 1999, when his career was in full flood with mainstream styling work for Seat, Fiat, Hyundai, Alfa Romeo, Daewoo and others, Giorgetto Giugiaro was named Designer of the 20th Century by a panel of 120 international experts. Each year his company was startling motor-show attendees with its imaginative and provocative prototypes. An offshoot organization, Giugiaro Design, was designing products from yachts to pots and pasta.

The astonishingly broad and deep contributions to design of Giorgetto Giugiaro derive from the intellectual investment in design that he has made over a career lasting more than half a century. A reader of philoso-

Two of today's power-packed designs: the Alfa Romeo supercar of 1998 and the 2009 Namir, purportedly the fastest "green" car on the planet. Right: Master designer Giugiaro at 70.

phy, following the lead of Professor Colmo, Giugiaro has given deep thought to the underlying principles of his profession. To this he brings his invaluable experience gained in working with automakers in all parts of the world save America, with the notable exception of the DeLorean DMC-12.

This doesn't mean his clients are undemanding, quite the contrary. They expect short-order miracles from this renowned designer. "Many think that perhaps I am a magician," Giugiaro reflected to the author. "It's not that I arrive one morning and say, 'Okay, I have an idea.' I have to work for ideas! People say that I'm a lucky man because I arrive with an idea, wake up and have an idea! In fact, I feel like a worker, a builder. I put bricks in a wall, one upon the other, to build something. But people think that I do it all of a piece. A magician! Mandrake!"

SURVIVOR
Sport on three wheels is nothing new

S tart with the punch line: What we see is an 1899 Peugeot-De Dion-Bouton tricycle, living evidence of the French (automotive) Revolution, the least-likely survivor one can imagine and perhaps the world's oldest operating motor vehicle still in private hands. And the owner is surely the only man alive in the 21st century to have gotten road rash at the hands of a 19th-century vehicle. But first, some history.

BY ALLAN GIRDLER
PHOTOGRAPHY BY LARRY CRANE

Most accounts of motoring's pioneer days begin with the Germans, as in Otto Daimler, who fielded a sort-of motorcycle powered by an internal-combustion, four-stroke engine in 1885, followed the next year by a four-wheeled gasoline-propelled car. But, current research shows that a team of French inventors and an American engineer, working separately, were riding steam-powered motorcycles – as in two wheels fore and aft, handlebars and twist grips – in 1868 or 1869.

France, otherwise known as the "Land of the Rising Soufflé," is where the breakthroughs came from; witness that when the Anglophone world took an interest, they adopted words such as transmission, chassis, chauffeur, garage, suspension and even automobile from the French. (Elsewhere on these pages is a theory as to why those machines of the 1860s were forgotten while the pioneers of the 1880s made the history books.)

First among the French pioneers was Comte Albert de Dion, an aristocrat, a man of force and influence, a scientist and a visionary. He was partnered with Georges Bouton, an engineer who could make what de Dion imagined and financed.

They first worked with steam. Legend says that when they were told there were no boilers small and efficient enough to power a vehicle, de Dion said: "Well then, we'll have to invent one," which they did.

The 1880s were a time of major progress, what with pneumatic rubber tires and bicycles with coaster hubs and, yes, boilers small enough to be mounted between wheels. And what of the public? People don't like change, as a rule, even change whose time has come, leading one social critic to write in 1888, "Any member of the public so divorced from all reason or sense of decency as to want a horseless carriage" could get one.

But de Dion et Bouton (written sometimes that way, other times with a hyphen) learned steam has its limits. It was too much bother getting under way and maintaining power was difficult, so they decided to work with internal combustion. Before you could say "Marchons" (We're going), they had a single-cylinder, air-cooled, four-stroke engine.

Meanwhile, other French innovators, including Peugeot, had practically mastered development of the bicycle and the tricycle, devising chain and coaster hubs among other elements. After some experiments with multiple cylinders and water cooling – de Dion took out a patent on the latter – the firm determined to build drivetrains to be installed in conjunction with frames and accoutrements from bicycle makers – hence the Peugeot-De Dion-Bouton partnership.

The rivals, mainly German, were building bulky engines with water tanks and very rudimentary mixing devices with ignition by flame, as in valves and doors. Bouton went electric with batteries, coil and timer. It worked and, not only that, the ignition system allowed

After some experiments with complex systems, de Dion (who held a patent on a form of water cooling) and Bouton decided to work with bicycle makers and from their strengths: powerplants and drivetrains. Hence the partnership.

for 3000 rpm in comparison to 750 rpm from the others. It was the first such high-speed engine, and it set the pattern for a generation. When Hendee and Hedstrom created the Indian Motocycle (another French spelling), and Harley and Davidson built its first engine, they used the De Dion Bouton as a template.

As for the original version, De Dion et Bouton experimented, modified and compromised, and by 1895 they had a small 50x70mm engine, which ran reliably at 1500 rpm, producing 0.5 horsepower. It

was attached to an ordinary pedal tricycle below and behind the saddle and drove the differential rear axle. Road tests in December 1895, with the stylishly stout count at the controls, recorded a road speed of 18 mph, and the need to apply pedal power uphill.

The stage was set. The engine was enlarged; partners and suppliers were signed up. There were variations; at first, a passenger trailer or delivery box for towing behind the tricycle, but mostly, the Count's goals of efficiency, convenience and agility were met with the tricycle seen here.

Next came sport: The tricycle was the sports car, perhaps even the sprint car, of its day. De Dion had competed with steam wagonettes. For instance, its entry was the fastest vehicle in the 1895 Paris-Bordeaux race, but, quoting a history of the marque, "What really impressed the enthusiasts was the performance of the little De Dion-Bouton petrol tricycles. In the motorcycle class in Marseilles-Nice-La Turbie, De Dion trikes finished first, second, fourth, fifth, sixth and seventh out of eight entrants … the pattern was consistently repeated until the turn of the century." Then, the big cars got lighter, the small cars got more power and sport became motorcycles.

The result? In the long run and wide view, the gasoline-powered three-wheeler – from Morgans through the Davis and Reliant cars to Mini Coopers posing as sidecar-hauling motorcycles, to Harley's now-forgotten Tri-Hawk to the Bombardier – has been reinvented time after time, but has never quite made it back into the mainstream.

A SAGA OF SURVIVAL

Now comes the long and narrow view, the history of the trike seen here. Owner Larry Feece, whose day job involves plastic injection molding, found someone with access to De Dion's factory records, and, according to the serial number on the engine, his trike was assembled in May 1899. There were no build sheets or registration records back then, so the next 20-odd years are lost to history.

Above: Larry Feece as a teen (far left), looking at the Bendix/Fitterling collection with his dad. The Peugeot is in the center. Below: the unrestored, 110-year-old machine started easily and ran perfectly for the time we ran it back and forth for photography.

But then came Vincent Bendix, who invented the Bendix drive, which made practical the electric starter that in turn made the automobile available to all. Bendix was an inventor, tycoon and an interesting man. Legend says that in 1922, Bendix and his dad were visiting Chicago when the latter was killed by a car that couldn't stop in time. Bendix vowed to correct this. He began research and went to France, where the engineers were still in the forefront of development.

While there, Bendix hired a French engineer and also bought the Peugeot-De Dion-Bouton seen here and in exactly the same condition. Look at the front wheel. Cars and motorcycles didn't get front-wheel brakes until the 1920s, yet here's a motorized tricycle with a front brake in 1899.

Bendix was a sportsman, drove elegant cars, flew airplanes and so forth, but Feece points out that the engine's primary gears are polished but not worn, while the front brake lining had seen heavy use. Bendix brought the tricycle home for research into brakes, and there in Bendix's shop it sat, preserved but not ridden or even run, according to the records.

The shop was in South Bend, Ind., which was home to another wealthy sportsman, trucking company owner Homer Fitterling, who at one time owned the largest

collection of Duesenbergs (37) in private hands. Bendix got himself into financial trouble and had to sell his company, plant, mansion, art collection and all of his cars, airplanes and other vehicles, enabling Fitterling to scoop up the trike. One can only guess as to why, because Fitterling didn't ride it much, either.

Fitterling was an outgoing man who enjoyed sharing his collection with other car nuts, one of whom was Larry Feece's dad. Luckily for Feece, he had the kind of father who took the kid with him on trips to Fitterling's garage. Feece was 12 or so and

fell totally, permanently and hopelessly in love with the De Dion-Bouton trike. Fitterling, who had only daughters, let the kid hang out and help around the garage. As the years passed, Feece became a Corvette expert and took part in restoring 'Vettes for Fitterling's collection. And during all that time, as you'd suspect, Feece repeatedly asked to buy the trike, but the owner always said no.

In 1982, Fitterling realized his daughters were interested in their inheritance and not in their dad's old cars. He told Feece the trike was for sale and named a price. How much? "It was more money than I had," Feece said. "I had to sell some other toys, but I came up with the money."

The remarkable engine used a detachable combustion chamber with an automatic inlet valve at the top, a mechanically opened exhaust valve at the bottom and a very modern-looking spark plug. The magic was the fuel/air-mixing carburetor with float control.

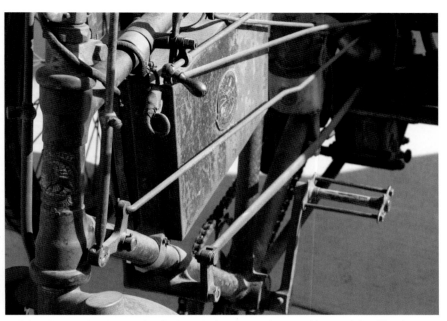

Above left: The carburetor with bottom fuel feed to the float chamber. On either side of the throttle body are the fuel and air mixture levers. Above right: The battery box hangs below the top tube. Below left: The brake levers are below the handgrips: front brake on right and rear on left. Large lever behind top tube makes the gear change; on the near side are the timing lever (vertical) and compression release (horizontal). The matching pair of vertical levers adjust fuel and air for carburetor. Below right: There are so few miles on the machine the gears still have mill marks.

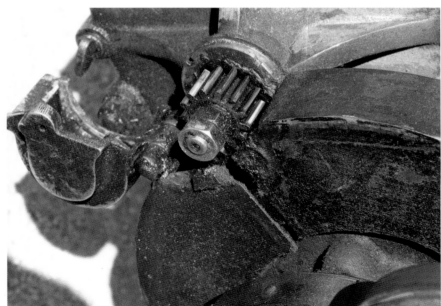

There was one more narrow escape for the trike: Feece's machine shop caught fire. It was nearly destroyed, but one corner of the building where the De Dion-Bouton was stored, protected only by an old blanket, was spared. "It wasn't supposed to be gone," said Feece.

What Will She Do?

Gearheads of all ages could spend hours looking at the details of this survivor. Because production was limited and there were many small suppliers, probably no two motorcycles from this time were exactly alike.

In this case, Peugeot bicycle parts comprise the frame, front forks and other cycle bits. The wheels are fitted with Dunlop brand tires, made under license in France. Each tire's sidewall is decorated with a portrait of Dunlop himself and, even now, the details are so sharp one can discern his whiskers.

The bicycle pedals and sprocket are one-way, i.e., the rider pedals and the trike goes forward, but when the engine or gravity take over, the pedals disengage. The left side of the front wheel sports a foot peg that functions as the dead pedal, a place for the operator to brake against cornering or braking forces.

Both brakes are hand operated through a carefully designed, spring-loaded linkage on the handlebars; the only part missing 108 years later is the spark control on the left-side grip. Speaking of details, cables were still in the future, so the wiring for the ignition was snugged to the frame rails by wraps of waxed string that are still in place today.

For detail extremes, look first at the ignition points cover: Rather than use a lock washer, Bouton's team used half a wing nut with the heavy half on the right, so that every jounce kept the nut tight. And look at the top of the axle: See those serrated bosses on each side? That's where the passenger stands, with arms presumably wrapped tight around the operator. (Other versions of these vehicles towed the passenger in a two-wheeled cart aft or plunked him or her in a seat in front of the rider, a 19th-century collapsible steering column, as it were.) Getting ahead, Feece was parading the trike on an oval track and lured his then-girlfriend into hopping aboard. Her hands around his neck, he said, gave new meaning to the words "throttle control."

Looking at Bouton's 1899 engine is like watching a Shakespeare play and realizing where all those familiar quotes originated. It features an upright cylinder,

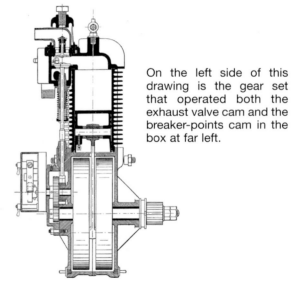

On the left side of this drawing is the gear set that operated both the exhaust valve cam and the breaker-points cam in the box at far left.

air cooled by fins, with the intake over the exhaust valve. The intake valve is pulled open when the piston goes down and is held closed by compression on the compression stroke and a light spring on the exhaust stroke. The exhaust valve is controlled by a one-lobe camshaft.

Ignition is by points, coil and batteries; the latter originals are a total loss. The trike arrived at Feece's shop with a set of French batteries that were lost in the fire mentioned earlier; they were replaced with modern lantern batteries that fit inside the box slung beneath the frame's top tube. The fuel tank is, of course, mounted below and aft of the seat. That little round cap, which looks like the oil pump on a 1920s motorcycle, is the fuel valve – twist to open.

The float-regulated carburetor is one of the very first of such developments; even such an expert antiquarian as the late Bud Ekins needed to see the records before he believed it was an 1899 component. And, even though it was a major improvement over having a box of gas with air pulled across it, this carb is basic.

There is no throttle; instead, there is an air valve and a fuel valve, both set while underway, with the engine

Above: The passenger compartment was a pair of toothy steel grips upon which to stand astraddle the engine. Below the beam is the ignition coil.

and vehicle speed controlled by spark advance setting and the gearbox. There are two speeds, high and low, with neutral, predicting federal mandate, placed between them. Note that there is no clutch. Drive goes from the crankshaft to the primary driven gear to the transmission and then to the differential. The engine can be disengaged from the transmission, but it can't be engaged when the engine is running.

There are brake levers, air and fuel valves, compression release, spark setting, gear shift and kill switch, making for eight controls, seven of which are worked during operation, all by hand. Literature of the day claimed that even ladies could handle these machines and, perhaps, relative to the complexity of a steam-driven car or cumbersome gas buggy, they could.

There is no way to know what happened to this trike during its first ownership, but by the lack of wear and tear, it can't have been ridden hard or put away wet. We know that Bendix did mostly research and Fitterling

collected more than he rode. Plus, after every operation, the fuel and oil were drained from their respective tanks. There have never been conditions that allowed sludge, varnish and such to build up in the engine, while the batteries are easily replaced or recharged. Feece estimates he's run the engine for perhaps six or seven hours during his 25 years of ownership. In sum, what we have here is a genuine, low-mileage motor tricycle not even ridden only on Sundays.

Why not? Because an 1899 motorized tricycle is neither easy nor risk free. Feece has fallen off, or maybe out, with no damage to the trike and only scrapes and bruises to himself, but this is not something to ride to the store, which gets us to the winding dirt road at the east end of a farming settlement, a location picked because nobody comes here, and especially not the sheriff.

The drill: Feece turns on the fuel, un-shorts the kill switch, tickles the float control, guesses at the air and fuel valves, opens the compression release, engages low gear and puts pedal to the chain. He reaches walking speed and closes the compression release. There's a chuff, then a pop; the engine is running and gaining speed as Feece sits down and juggles the carb levers.

You had to see it *not* to believe it. We're talking 400 cc or so and maybe 3 bhp with a top speed of 35 mph. There is no smoke, no stutter, just an even, strong pop-pop-pop of a four-stroke single. Amazing stuff, but remember: Federal do-gooders hounded the three-wheel ATVs out of production. Bendix studied these brakes, he didn't copy them, and there is no clutch.

Feece flips the lever into neutral and the engine dies. He turns it around, engages the gearbox, and back he comes. In this corner of the world, it's 1899 all over again and we gearheads are the better, and more humble, for it.

The creation of the pneumatic tire empowered development of really useful motor vehicles. The tear-drop-shaped box on the left of the crankcase contains Georges Bouton's cam – operated contact breaker; the invention that permitted reliably timed spark up to 3000 crankshaft rpm – and the future of internal combustion.

THE MISSING LINK

Read the latest accounts of motorized history, and you'll learn that Sylvester Roper, an engineer whose day job was at the Springfield, Mass., armory, was trundling around the Boston area in a steam-powered wagon and that Roper and a French team of inventors independently built steam-driven motorcycles in 1868 or 1869.

Read earlier historical accounts and Otto Daimler is credited with building a motorcycle – more like a test bed for his engine with two wheels fore and aft, plus training wheels at each side – followed by a four-wheeler, an automobile, in 1886.

How can this be? And why did it take a generation for motorcars and motorbikes to become mainstream? Why didn't those first true pioneers leave a mark? For the same reason those Viking and Celtic voyages to the Americas had no effect on recorded history, and Columbus gets his own national holiday. There is no sum until you have all the parts.

The missing link? Pneumatic rubber tires with carcass and inner tube.

We have here a triangle: At mid-19th century, we had railroads and canals for moving heavy freight with wagons, buggies and coaches pulled by horses at a walking pace. The "tire" of the day was an iron or steel strap wrapped around a wheel with wood spokes and rim. Roads were dirt or gravel with narrow tracks. There were cobblestones in the cities, and coaches and large wagons had crude springs between body and axle. The metal tires had no give or trip, but that didn't matter because the horses didn't go fast, which meant the roadbed could be, and was, rough and rutted. In short, those self-propelled pioneer vehicles used solid metal "tires" of the day and traveled bad roads; the power to out-pull and out-run a horse got them nothing.

Next is one of those perfect ironies. Charles Goodyear learned how to vulcanize rubber in 1844, making it into a useful industrial material. Robert Thompson, a Scot, devised the first pneumatic tire in 1845. He was awarded a patent, but his method was complicated and expensive, and the roads and vehicles were so limited, there was no reason to use the flexible, shock-absorbing, traction-granting tire. The patent fell into obscurity.

Then, John Dunlop, who hadn't heard of Thompson but who complained of headaches because his bicycle rode so roughly, reinvented the tire. Because no one else had heard of Thompson, either, Dunlop was granted a patent in 1888.

Timing is everything. Right on the heels of Daimler's test bed and pioneer motorcar came pneumatic tires for bicycles and motorcycles. Michelin made the first car tire, followed by the Schrader valvestem and the clincher rim, both of which allowed motorists to patch and pump at the roadside.

Think computers are fast? Consider the incrementally, instantly flexible tire, yielding here and pushing back there, shaping itself to the ruts and ripples of a muddy path while isolating the vehicle and its occupants from the jolts and slams that until then had slowed vehicular progress to the pace of a horse. Connect those two other dots and the wheeled vehicle can outpace the horse, allowing more horsepower and justifying improved roads and highways. "Get a horse" becomes "Gentlemen, start your engines."

As for history: Once the world took notice, someone dug up Thompson's patent, and Dunlop's was cancelled. But, as time teaches us, you can't stop a sum when all the parts are in place.

The science of horsepower versus weight. Ettore Bugatti put two engines on his racing tricycle; some mounted three.

THE THREE JEWELS OF THE TRIDENT

The Brothers Maserati were perpetually strapped financially, but never bankrupt where engineering talent was concerned. Would their new car be a winner, or just another "also ran"?

BY L. SPENCER RIGGS

From the early days of the 20th century, the Maserati brothers – Alfieri, Bindo, Carlo and Ernesto – were involved in the production of automobiles. After developing the Diatto 2-liter Grand Prix cars and the Maserati the V8RI earlier in their careers, Maserati began concentrating exclusively on the voiturette class. Soon thereafter, new Grand Prix rules took effect in 1938 dictating that engine capacities must be held to only 3-liter supercharged and 4.5 liters normally aspirated. The change in formula caused Maserati, Bugatti and Delahaye to join Alfa-Romeo in trying to defeat the two German giants. Ernesto was soon at work on a handsome 3-liter supercharged Grand Prix car he called the 8CTF. The type designation came from 8 cilindi testa fissa, or 8-

and-stroke arrangement was 2.700 x 3.900. Various displacement figures are given for these engines, but the bore-and-stroke figures measure out to 178.5 cubic inches. However, given that possible experimentation may have taken place over the years, some of these engines may have been honed or "cleaned out" to 181, or as much as 182.5 cid. Horsepower figures are given as 350 to 360 at 6300 to 6500 rpm. Instead of the usual Borgo pistons, Ernesto ordered specially crafted Issota-Fraschini slugs, which were finish-machined by the Maserati works. Compression was 6.5 to 1. Twin positive-displacement Roots superchargers, one turned by the crankshaft, the other geared to a camshaft, provided 17 psi. Each blower fed four cylinders, providing instant acceleration. Twin Memini MA12

The engine was dropped into a very rigid box-section rail frame, which was a longer-wheelbase version of the successful 6CM 1.5-liter chassis. Factory figures give the racer a wheelbase of 107.1 inches. The frame rails were joined together at the rear by a huge magnesium casting that also served as an oil tank, holding approximately eight gallons. The chassis was also braced by large cross-members. The center of gravity was astonishingly low for the era and permitted by use of a torque tube drive connected to a spur gear step-up on the nose of the rear axle. The rear suspension utilized quarter-elliptic leaf springs and friction shocks backed up by adjustable hydraulic units. The front wishbone suspension was independently sprung via torsion bars and lateral links with friction dampers.

Above: Start of the 1938 Tripoli Grand Prix finds the all-Mercedes front row of Hermann Lang #46, Manfred von Brauchitsch #44, Rudi Caracciola #46, with Achille Varzi in 8CTF Maserati #10 high against the wall and Count Trossi (center of photo) in the other 8CTF. Trossi overhauled everyone and led several laps before retiring with mechanical trouble. Right: Villoresi fights to control his 8CTF Maserati during his fierce charge through the field in the 1938 Donington Grand Prix. He was running fifth amidst the Mercedes and Auto Unions when a broken piston ended his day. By this point, chassis 3030 was equipped with the new side panels and streamlined suspension bodywork.

cylinder fixed head.

The straight-eight engine for the 8CTF was derived from two cast-iron 4-cylinder 4CM engines utilizing a common crankshaft and crankcase. The steel crankshaft ran in five plain bearings. The integral double-overhead cam head contained two valves per cylinder set at an included angle of 90 degrees. The bore-

carburetors mounted directly on the superchargers handled high-octane gasoline. The mixture was fired by a single Scintilla Vertex magneto. The normal firing order was 1-7-3-2-8-4-6. However, on the final machine produced, the Boyle Maserati, the firing order was changed to 1-3-6-8-4-2-7-5 in order to obtain smoother performance.

The unsprung weight was very low, and the rigid frame enabled the car to stick like glue in the turns. Steering was by worm-and-sector.

The dry multidisc clutch, six Ferodo composite and five steel, sent power to the transmission. The transmission, which owed its origins to the 8CM, was integral with the engine. Possessing four speeds for-

Above: Paul Pietsch in the pits for one of many stops he made during the running of the 1939 German Grand Prix. Nevertheless, at one point he led the race, finishing an incredible third. This is chassis 3031. Right: Ace mechanic Cotton Henning (in white hat) appears to be taking a spark plug reading, while Wilbur Shaw (in helmet and goggles) looks over Cotton's shoulder, during Indy practice in 1939. Spark plugs were always a major concern for the Maserati.

ward and reverse, it was operated by a central gearshift between the driver's knees.

The braking system on these cars was a tremendous factor in their performance. The huge 16-inch magnesium drum brakes, hydraulically actuated, with special high-temperature lining on iron shoes, allowed drivers to go deep into the turns. The master cylinder was from the Fiat Ardita. However, it was later replaced in favor of a larger, more efficient Lockheed unit.

Wire wheels of 3.25 x 19 up front and 4.00 x 19 rear, mounting Pirelli tires of 5.50 forward and 6.00 x 19 or optional 6.50 x 19 aft, was standard fare. However, when the cars came to America, their new owners employed larger Firestone tires.

The beautiful hand-formed aluminum bodywork made for a striking, esthetically pleasing machine. The entire car weighed only 780 kg, or approximately 1,718 pounds.

Testing of the first engine was done on Jan. 20, 1938. Shortly thereafter – the exact dates vary – the first car designated chassis no. 3030 was tested on a straightaway run at Navicello. All the Maserati dignitaries were on hand, and test driver Guerino Bertocchi was in the cockpit. Tests were so successful that a second machine, designated chassis no. 3031, was completed on May 4.

The original car, chassis 3030, had a smooth, uninterrupted hood line around the exhaust headers, plus a cutaway area for the pitman arm. Both cars had twin exhaust pipes on the left side. And while they appeared to be identical, there were ways to identify them from one another. The second car, chassis 3031, was identifiable by a small hood flap that fitted between the two exhaust headers. The second car also had a prominent "bump" in the bodywork just below the exhaust headers to accommodate travel of the pitman arm. (Most of the bodywork described was not added until the winter of 1938-39.)

On May 15, 1938, the two gleaming red racers, with Count Carlo Felice Trossi assigned to 3031 and Achille Varzi in 3030, were entered in the Tripoli Grand Prix. Both cars qualified for the second row, with Trossi the slightly faster of the two. After four circuits of the race, Trossi ripped through the field to take the lead from Hermann Lang's Mercedes. The spectators and the Maserati pits turned handsprings when Trossi turned the fastest lap of the race on the eighth circuit.

Trossi continued to pull away from Lang, Giuseppe Farina's Alfa-Romeo, and the Mercedes of Rudi Caracciola. With 11 circuits of the 40-lap distance complete, Varzi coasted to the pits with final drive failure. He was never a factor.

Trossi's engine began to sound rough; he fell back and lost the lead to Lang. At 15 laps, Trossi retired with engine and rear axle trouble.

Although the new cars failed to finish, their speed, which was at least equal to the new V12 Mercedes W154s, was obvious. And even if Caracciola considered the 8CTF to be an inferior car (see AQ Vol. 49 No. 1), he apparently forgot, at least for a while, that he started the 1938 season looking at the tail of one. And it wouldn't be the last time the champion would look at the tail of an 8CTF.

Apparently, both 8CTFs suffered from overheating at Tripoli. When they appeared on Aug. 7 at Livorno for the Coppa Ciano, the air inlets for the radiator in

Above: A very interesting photo of Cotton Henning, with Wilbur Shaw seated in the Maserati in the Indy garage area in early 1946. The new tail with headrest faring and additional bodywork, made necessary by Shaw's accident in 1941, are evident. The 8CTF still carries the famous prewar maroon color and Shaw deuce. Subsequently, it would be painted a light purple and white for the '46 race. Above right: The former Boyle Maserati torn down for inspection prior to the 1947 Indy classic. This clearly shows the larger tail and the headrest installed by Cotton Henning. Note the parallel torsion bars on the front suspension. Below: Standing in the Maserati's cockpit, Wilbur Shaw kisses his wife Boots in Victory Lane, following his second straight and third overall Indy win. The news media is hanging on his every word. Note the traditional milk jug in Wilbur's right hand and the wire enclosure around the winner's circle. Racers dubbed it "the bullpen."

the nose were considerably larger. By this juncture, Varzi had been dropped from the team in favor of Goffredo "Freddie" Zehender, who took over chassis 3030. Trossi was at the wheel of 3031. At every practice session, Trossi recorded the fastest lap. He sent the Italian fans into cheers when he took the pole position with a time of 2:26. Although Caracciola succeeded in equaling Trossi's lap, the Count had turned the trick first. Thus, he won the pole. Zehender was in row two.

In the race, Trossi got off to a bad start but salvaged fourth at the end of the first lap behind Caracciola, Lang and Farina. By the fourth lap, Zehender's 8CTF was out with engine trouble; on that same lap, Trossi fought his way around Caracciola into the lead. The 8CTF began pulling away from the field, but on the eighth lap, Trossi pulled into the pits with engine trouble.

The Maserati connections had been so hopeful, but many people close to the sport felt the cars were underprepared. Old habits die hard. The Maserati brothers had always surrounded themselves with a small group of trusted technicians to prepare their racers. Coupled with their almost-constant participation in 1500cc racing, the staff was often spread too thin.

A week later, the team was at Pescara for the Coppa Acerbo. Chassis 3031, with Trossi at the wheel, could only manage a place in the last row. Throughout practice an ignition misfire seemed to be the problem. Voiturette driver Luigi Villoresi was assigned to 3030. However, the car was still under repair in Maserati's Bologna shops and never arrived in Pescara.

In the race, Trossi made little headway, even though the 8CTF appeared to be running well. For some time, Trossi had been very ill with the disease that would eventually end his life. Feeling far from fit, after only a few laps on the huge course, he handed over to Villoresi.

Far behind the field with no hope of winning, Villoresi threw all caution to the wind. His blazing speed on the engine-rending straights was amazing. And his lock-to-lock slides through the towns caused the populace to wonder if Tazio Nuvolari was behind the wheel. Twice he broke the outright lap record, but on lap 10 of the 16-lap race, his brilliant charge toward the front ended when the Maserati suffered engine trouble.

On Sept. 8, 1938, construction was completed on a third 8CTF, designated chassis no. 3032. This machine differed from the others in that it had a single exhaust pipe, hydraulic shocks only on the rear and the aforementioned different firing order.

Above: Horn and Bergere have already gone by the camera, but Rose, Snowberger in the Federal Engineering Maserati and Bill Holland lead the rest of the field into turn one at the start of the '47 Indy 500. Right: During 1948 Indy practice, the crew is about to check over the Bennett Brothers'-sponsored Maserati, with Ted Horn in the cockpit. Chief mechanic Cotton Henning (white shirt, center of group) is leaning in to hear what Ted has to say about the car's performance.

TRIPLE THREAT

On Oct. 11, all three 8CTFs were at Monza for the Italian GP. Villoresi was in 3030, Trossi in 3031 and Zehender in the new 3032. Driving a much more subdued race than normal, Trossi ran just off the pace and finished fifth. Unfortunately, he was later disqualified for receiving mechanical help outside the pit area. Villoresi retired about midrace with unspecified mechanical trouble. Zehender crashed the new car through some sandbags and hay bales at a chicane, with little or no damage.

At the Donington Grand Prix, on Oct. 22, Villoresi made a tremendous drive with 8CTF 3030. He got away to a poor start but came charging through the field as though the forests of Donington were his home track. On lap 16, he forced the Maserati around Manfred von Brauchitsch's Mercedes, to take fifth place. Running amid the Mercedes and Auto Unions,

Villoresi went after the leaders. He was homing in on them when a broken piston ended his gallant run.

The mechanical failures were a huge disappointment to the Maserati brothers, but they could take solace in that 8CTF 3031, in every event in which it took part, either set the fastest lap in practice or in the race itself – a remarkable feat.

Over the winter, few changes were made to the cars performance-wise. However, all three were equipped with all-enveloping, louvered side panels and additional streamlining around the suspension, as already described. This included closing in the pitman and steering-arm mechanism.

Meanwhile, in America, Wilbur Shaw had driven one of the V8RI Maseratis in the Vanderbilt Cup race. While the diminutive Shaw realized the car wasn't a world-beater, the handling and the brakes impressed him. According to Shaw, he spoke with Mike Boyle, who fielded cars at Indy. Shaw said he'd guarantee an Indy victory if Boyle would purchase a later model GP

car. Boyle apprized his ace mechanic Cotton Henning of Shaw's idea.

Henning, a savvy wrench-twister, strode through Gasoline Alley and purchased a Maserati sight unseen. However, when the car arrived, it was a 91cid 6CM – not at all what Shaw had envisioned. Shaw took one

practice ride in the car and quickly went back to his '37 Indy-winning Gilmore Special.

In February 1939, Henning traveled to Italy, where he purchased the "new" 8CTF chassis 3032. On arrival in Indianapolis, Shaw and Henning discovered that the Maserati mechanics had forgotten to drain water from the engine blocks. In transit, they had frozen and cracked. According to both men, they had to await the arrival of a new engine from Italy. Although there was no chassis no. 3033, this new engine carried that identifying numeral.

When engine 3033 was eventually nestled in chassis 3032, even though it was below freezing in Indy, Wilbur couldn't resist taking a few practice laps in the 8CTF. The red beauty was everything Shaw hoped it would be. He soon ripped off four laps against Henning's stopwatch at more than 127 mph, about 2 mph over the existing track record.

However, Henning was soon apprised of all the historical breakdowns suffered by the 8CTFs, including engine failures and especially connecting-rod trouble. The answer: raise the gear ratio, use larger 20-inch tires on the rear and keep the revs well below the red-lined 6500 rpm. Of course, this hurt the Maserati's top speed, but it was a necessary sacrifice.

There was also the now well-known story of how the spark plugs would "glaze over" when methanol fuel was used. At such times, the engine refused to start. Henning solved the problem by installing a small tank filled with gasoline in the cowl. Shaw switched to gasoline whenever the engine was going to be shut off, and that solved the problem. During May practice, the rear main bearing seal developed an oil leak. The engine was running so well, Cotton didn't want to tear it down for a minor problem. He decided to install a six-gallon auxiliary oil tank so the racer would have enough oil for the race.

These and other subtle little "Henningizations" were kept secret, but the performance of chassis 3032 would not be lost on the racing world.

In May 1939, Shaw qualified the maroon Maserati at 128.977 mph, claiming the outside position on Indy's front row. Jimmy Snyder, in one of the Thorne-Sparks' "Little Sixes," took the pole with a new record of 130.138. Shaw's buddy and three-time Indy champ Louie Meyer and his straight-eight Winfield-powered Bowes Seal Fast Special were in the middle of row one at 130.067.

From the drop of the flag, the three front-row starters swapped the lead in a thrilling duel. Late in the race, it looked as if Meyer was on his way to an unprecedented fourth Indy win. "I was hanging on for dear life," Meyer said. "All through our duels, Wilbur was driving through the turns with one hand, thumbing his nose at me. He'd jump on those big brakes and accelerate right away from me with those Roots blowers. I had speed on him down the straights, so did Snyder. But when we got to the turns – anytime [Shaw] wanted to – he could drive right away from us.

"But there was one place I had it on Wilbur," Meyer continued. "I had a bigger fuel tank, and his Maserati was pretty thirsty."

Meyer had a lap on Shaw, but the big Bowes job blew a right front tire. By the time Meyer limped to the pits, changed the tire and returned to the track, Shaw had taken the lead. Even so, with only a few laps remaining, Meyer was gaining on Shaw, but with two

Louis Unser ready to take his turn against the clock at Pikes Peak in 1949. This time, Unser and Dick Cott's Maserati had to settle for second place. This is the Maserati-powered chassis no. 3030, the very first 8CTF produced.

laps to go, Meyer lost control and crashed coming out of turn two. The car hit the inside rail, jumped into the air and threw Meyer out. He was unhurt.

Shaw and the Maserati took the checkered flag, ending a dramatic race.

During the 1939 Grand Prix season the other two 8CTFs weren't entered in a race until the German Grand Prix on July 23. Villoresi was assigned to chassis 3030; German driver Paul Pietsch handled 3031. With his knowledge of the Nurburgring, Pietsch started from row three alongside the latest Auto Unions of Nuvolari and Hans Stuck. Villoresi was in the fifth row.

Race day was cloudy and cold with the Nurburgring mist covering most of the course. On the opening lap, Lang took a long lead from von Brauchitsch, who was followed by Hermann Muller, Caracciola, Nuvolari and Pietsch. Villoresi pitted at the end of the opening lap with spark plug trouble. Meanwhile, Pietsch was carving his way through the field with amazing speed.

By the time rain began to fall, Lang and Villoresi were out. In the end, Caracciola took the checkered flag 57.8 seconds ahead of Muller, with Pietsch finish-

ing an outstanding third.

The performance of the Maserati wasn't lost on Swiss-born Laury Schell, who had been watching the cars since their debut at Tripoli, in '38. Only days before the Swiss Grand Prix, he and his American wife Lucy O'Reilly Schell purchased 8CTFs nos. 3030 and 3031.

On Aug. 20 at the Swiss Grand Pix, Lucy installed defending French Auto Racing Champion Rene Dreyfus in 3031 and "Raph" in 3030. There had been little or no time to prepare the cars since the Schells had purchased them. Due to mechanical trouble, Raph didn't start.

The always-treacherous Bremgarten course was deadly in the wet, and for most of the race it rained buckets. Because he had witnessed one of Pietsch's spins in the rain in Germany, Dreyfus played it cautiously in order not to be caught out by the Maserati's lightning acceleration. He finished eighth. Lang was the winner.

Lucy Schell was determined to enter her cars in the 1940 Indy 500, with Dreyfus and Rene LeBegue as her drivers. Reportedly, in mid-September, well after World War II had started, Lucy somehow made her way to Modena, where she had the Maserati factory prepare the cars for Indy. Her husband, though, would never know of their fortunes.

On Oct. 18, 1939, the Schells were involved in a highway accident. Laury was killed instantly and Lucy badly injured. Somehow, Lucy managed to get the two Maseratis and their drivers to Indy in 1940.

Shaw put the Boyle Maserati in the middle of the front row with an average of 127.065 mph. Rex Mays, in the same Bowes Seal Fast entry that Meyer had driven in '39, took the pole at 127.850. Rose, in Lou Moore's Elgin Piston Pin dirt car, started on the outside at 125.624.

Meanwhile, LeBegue, in chassis 3030, narrowly made the race by qualifying at 118.981 mph. To be fair, because of the language barrier, the two Frenchman didn't understand Indy's qualifying rules. They presumed, as in Europe, that every car that arrived at the track would start the race. Dreyfus, making an effort to spare his car for the race, only clocked 118.831. He was bumped from the lineup. Later, just to show he could do better, Dreyfus turned laps in the 125 mph range before blowing his engine.

Early in the race, Shaw and Mays traded the lead, but neither one seemed to have a lasting advantage. Shaw would have to make two pit stops, while Mays, running on gasoline, could go through on one.

On lap 34, Shaw took command, and Mays seemed to be content to run second. Forty laps later, when Shaw pitted for fuel and tires, he had a 40-second advantage on Mays. But the Maserati's engine died, and it took some frantic cranking to refire the red-hot straight-eight. Shaw returned to the track running third to Mays and Rose, but when they all had cycled through their stops, Shaw was back in front. The weather began to be a factor as dark clouds came over the Speedway. Shaw put on a burst of speed and lapped the entire field.

On lap 144, the Maserati made her second and last stop of the day. Six laps later, it started to rain. The

Russ Snowberger, Paul Russo, Wilbur Shaw and car owner Dick Cott (left to right) pose beside the Federal Engineering Maserati entry at Indy in 1948. Shaw could always be found looking over any of the 8CTFs.

yellow flag came out, and the drivers held their positions while the light drizzle never let up. Shaw took the checkered flag to become the first driver in history to win back-to-back Indy races, and the Maserati became the first car to do so. Mays, Rose, Boyle teammate Ted Horn and Joel Thorne rounded out the top five.

The LeBegue-Dreyfus Maserati came home a creditable 10th. Dreyfus claimed they could have done even better had he not been black-flagged for passing under the yellow. Again, the Frenchman didn't understand American-track racing rules.

Lucy O'Reilly Schell saw the writing on the wall. With the world headed for war, she decided to sell the two Maseratis in the states. They were purchased for a fraction of their worth by Lou Moore.

IMMEDIATE PREWAR

In 1941, Shaw, Henning and the Boyle Maserati were cocked and primed to win three straight Indy classics. But Rose, wheeling Lou Moore's Maserati chassis 3031, took the pole with a four-lap average of 128.691 mph. Mays, in the familiar Bowes Seal Fast, was next at 128.301, with Shaw and the Boyle Maserati on the outside of row one at 127.836. Shaw remained nonchalant. Duke Nalon, in Moore's chassis 3030, barely made the race at 122.951. He started 30th.

A garage mechanic in his younger days, Shaw always insisted on balancing his own tires. He found one wheel and tire he couldn't keep balanced. He chalked on the side of the big Firestone: "OK-Bal-Use-Last." With as many sets as he balanced, he didn't think the tire would be needed.

On race-day morning, a mechanic's blowtorch touched off a fire that raged through the garages in Gasoline Alley. Only one car in the starting field was lost, but the firemen's hoses washed away all identification on the Maserati's tires.

On the starting line, the Boyle car refused to fire. Cotton spun the crank until he was ready to drop. The pit crew pushed for all they were worth. Finally, as other cars rushed by, at the last possible moment before the Maserati would have been disqualified, the engine fired. Wilbur took up his position, giving Rose and Mays a big grin. The three top qualifiers traded the lead in the opening laps, but Shaw shot by Mays, then blasted by Rose.

At 60 laps, Rose dropped out with spark plug trouble. Teammate Floyd Davis was running well back. Moore flagged Davis in, and Rose took to the cockpit, flogging the big blue-and-red dirt car back into the fray.

At 138 laps, leading by more than two minutes, Shaw pitted. The stop was routine, and he soon resumed cruising away from the field. The Maserati had the third 500-Mile Race in her sights. Yet on lap 152, heading into the main straight, Shaw felt the car waver slightly. He thought – he hoped – it might be a gust of wind, but when he set up for the first turn, some spokes in the right rear wheel parted with the hub. The

Maserati did a half-spin and smacked the outside wall tail first. The fuel tank ruptured, but there was no fire. The tank brace struck Wilbur's spine, and the shock of the blow paralyzed him for a few hours.

Shaw always believed the wheel he couldn't balance was the one that failed.

After all sorts of mechanical maladies, Nalon's Maserati was the only 8CTF running at the finish. He was flagged in 15th position, 27 laps behind the winning car shared by Rose and Davis.

POSTWAR AND BEYOND

In 1946, following WW II, Ted Horn inherited the Boyle Maserati from the retired Shaw. Wilbur was now president of the Indianapolis Motor Speedway. The Boyle car, 3032, now painted lavender and white, had a new tail with a headrest fairing that distinguished it from other 8CTFs and even the newer 8CLs. Although the latter had headrests resembling the Boyle, the 8CLs were shorter and more a part of the cockpit. Also, the grilles and the noses of the two types were shaped differently.

During Indy practice, Horn, like Shaw before him, was entranced by the power and roadholding of the Maserati. Horn qualified at a rather sedate 123.980 mph, but it was good enough to start seventh on the grid.

Dick Cott, the new owner of 3031, with Russ Snowberger at the wheel, qualified 10th at 121.591 mph. Former driver Frank Brisko had purchased 3030. Emil Andres qualified it in 11th place at 121.139.

On the opening lap of the race, Horn coasted to the pits with a dead magneto. With the pit crew caught unaware, and the red-hot supercharger supply tubes running right above the mag, Henning had quite a time making the switch. It took 13 minutes. When Horn returned to the track, he was seven laps behind the last place car.

Driving at an unbelievable pace, Horn kept coming through the field. This, and the high mechanical attrition of the field, enabled Horn to vault up the standings at a tremendous clip. Late in the race, his Maserati was turning the fastest laps of any car still running. At

Snowberger (goggles around neck), along with crew members and track officials, admire the Federal Engineering entry near Indy's famed Pagoda, in 1947. This is chassis 3031.

the finish, he was three laps down but still gaining on eventual winner George Robson when the checkered flag flew. Twelve minutes after Robson took the flag, the Boyle Maserati completed her 500 miles, finishing third. The 13 minutes for the swap cost Horn the race.

Showberger and Nalon, who took the wheel after 225 laps, were awarded 12th place. Andres in 8CTF 3030 finished fourth, his best Indy finish and the best Indy result for the veteran Brisko.

Installing perennial favorite Louie Unser in the cockpit, the cagy Snowberger took 3031 to the 1946 Pikes Peak Hill Climb. Unser and the screaming maroon-and-silver streak made a shambles of the competition. Their winning time of 15:28.7 for the historic climb, was a new record.

Indy 1947 found the former Boyle Maserati under the sponsorship of the Bennett brothers. Now carrying Horn's gold number one as the AAA National Driving Champion, and painted a gleaming black, the car was still wrenched and, at this time owned, by Henning.

Horn and the Maserati took the pole at 126.564 mph. Snowberger, who had fabricated an intercooler and installed it on 3031, started sixth at 121.331.

Brisko's 3030 wasn't entered.

In the opening laps, Horn ran second, 25 yards astern of leader Cliff Bergere in the vaunted Novi. So great was their speed, they were lapping cars by the seventh lap. Shortly thereafter, however, Horn unexpectedly pitted. Ted was covered with oil, and there was no apparent reason. Henning sent him back out, but a few laps more and the Maserati pitted again. Cotton discovered there was additional pressure building up in the reserve oil tank. A few minutes later, Horn was back in the race. In a near duplication of '46, the Maserati was seven laps behind the leader.

Meanwhile, for the first third of the race, Snowberger ran in the top five. He looked really strong behind the dueling trio of Bill Holland, Rose and Mays, but on lap 74, the Cott Maserati lost its oil pump and "Snowy's" run was over.

At 75 laps, Horn edged into the top 10. By half-distance, he was running sixth. At 122 laps, his Maserati challenged Bergere for fourth. The duel lasted 11 circuits and as Mays dropped out, Horn sailed by the Novi and into third place. Late in the race, Horn was 5 mph faster than any other car on the track, but it was too late. Rose won, with his Blue Crown teammate Holland taking second and Horn a fast closing third.

At Pikes Peak, Unser and Cott's 3031 once again claimed the hill climb victory. His time of 16:34.77 narrowly nipped Al Rogers' Coniff Offy.

The next year at Indy found Horn back in Henning's Maserati, qualifying fifth at 126.565. Many people picked the national champ to win the 500. Paul Russo in Cott's Maserati and Harry McQuinn in Brisko's 3030 started 25th and 26th, respectively. On the eve of the race, Henning found abrasive in the Maserati's oil system. Cotton did a quick rebuild of the engine, keeping the obvious sabotage a secret.

On race day, McQuinn only lasted a lap before one of his superchargers quit. Six laps later, Russo went out with an oil leak.

By the 10th circuit, Horn ran down Rose, Holland and Mays to take the lead. At 100 miles, Horn was still out front and lapped Nalon's Novi. At 150 miles, the black Maserati was averaging a record-setting 121.876 mph. She was breaking records for every distance, many of them set by her with Shaw at the wheel. The only time Horn relinquished the lead was when he pitted. Late in the event, while homing in on Rose, who was leading, Horn caught the oil pressure dropping. Even with Cotton's diligent work, they didn't get all the abrasive out of the intricate lubricating system. Ted backed off to an even 100 mph to save the rod bearings. He finished fourth behind Rose, Holland and Nalon.

A few weeks after the death of Ted Horn in his own dirt champ car at DuQuoin, Ill., Cotton Henning died of heart failure. Henning had ordered what he said was a "new" Maserati. In truth, it was the second 8CL, which had seen extensive use in South America. Maybe Henning meant the car was new to his team? In any event, his stable of Maseratis – the Boyle 8CTF chassis 3032 and the 8CL chassis 3035 – were pur-chased by a group of Indiana businessmen. The new team was called Indianapolis Race Cars, Inc.

In early May, the group hired ace mechanic Art Sparks to prepare the two cars. Sparks found both machines in many pieces scattered about a garage.

On the second weekend of Indy qualifications, Lee Wallard put the former Shaw car in the field at a surprising 128.912 mph, though he still had to start 20th. Freddie Agabashian and the 8CL barely made the show at 127.007.

In the race, Wallard came charging through the field, taking the lead from Mays on lap 36. For 19 glorious circuits, Wallard and the old Boyle car led the field, but on lap 55, the differential gave out. Agabashian had already dropped out with overheating. (Cott had purchased the Maserati 3030 for a two-car entry, but neither machine made the race.)

At Pikes Peak in '49, Unser spun 3030 right before the finish line. He took the checkered flag in reverse gear going backwards. He finished third. Snowberger, in the Maserati/Offy 3031, was seventh.

Spring and midget star Joe Barzda acquired the two Cott Maseratis in the early '50s. From 1951-53 Barzda and other drivers strove to make the Indy lineup, but they never came close to qualifying.

When the Indianapolis Motor Speedway's (IMS) first Hall of Fame Museum was erected, the Boyle Maserati was one of the first cars purchased for restoration. Arguably the most successful car in Indy history, Maserati 8CTF 3032 holds a special place in the hallowed hall at IMS.

Chassis 3030 passed through many hands until it found a home with Dean Butler in Cincinnati. Today, it's undergoing a complete restoration in the shops of Phil Reilly and Company for her current owner, the fabulous Collier Museum in Florida. Chassis 3031 is owned by Joel Finn and is impeccably turned out in her original Maserati red.

All three of these tremendous machines have appeared at various motor racing events and shows around the world. Amazingly, they have survived to bear testimony that they truly are the three jewels of the trident. ◢◣

Indy 1950 found one of Dick Cott's Maserati's sponsored by local car dealer Fadely-Anderson. Veteran sprint car star "Spider" Webb was at the wheel. Russ Snowberger had converted this car, chassis 3031, to Offenhauser power. Note the new hood without louvers and the cut-out to accommodate the Offy's sidedraft carburetors.

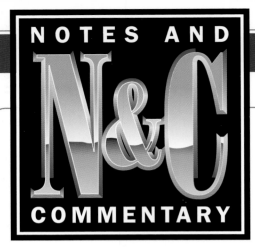

NOTES AND N&C COMMENTARY

VOLUME 49 NO.3

CONTACTING AQ

Automobile Quarterly, ISSN 0005-1438, ISBN: 1-59613-063-6 (978-1-59613-063-0), is published quarterly by Automobile Heritage Publishing and Communications, LLC. Editorial and publication offices: 800 East 8th Street, New Albany, Indiana, USA 47150. Telephone (812) 948-AUTO (2886); fax (812) 948-2816; e-mail info@autoquarterly.com; Web site www. autoquarterly.com.

SUBSCRIPTION SERVICE

For subscriptions, back issues, indexes, reader service, changes of address, and order entry, call (866) 838-2886. If calling from Indiana or outside the U.S., call (812) 948-2886. Back issue prices start at $25.95, plus shipping. For domestic subscription orders: 1 year (4 issues), $79.95; 2 years (8 issues), $149.95; 3 years (12 issues), $199.95. For Canadian orders: 1 year, $99.95; 2 years, $189.95; 3 years, $259.95. For all other international orders: 1 year, $109.95; 2 years, $209.95; 3 years, $289.95. Mastercard, Visa, or American Express are accepted. Order online at www.autoquarterly.com. To order by mail, please send check or money order to *AQ/Automobile Quarterly*, 1950 Classic Car Circle, P.O. Box 1950, New Albany, IN 47151. The fax number for orders is (812) 948-2816.

POSTMASTER

Please send all changes of address to: *Automobile Quarterly*, P.O. Box 1950, New Albany, IN 47151. Periodical postage paid at New Albany, Indiana, and at additional mailing offices.

LEGAL NOTICE

Entire contents copyright 2009 by Automobile Heritage Publishing and Communications, LLC. Library of Congress Catalog Number 62-4005. *AQ, Automobile Quarterly*, Quatrafoil, and  are registered trademarks of Automobile Heritage Publishing and Communications, LLC. All rights reserved. Reproduction in whole or in part without permission is prohibited.

OPPORTUNITY

Details of fund-raising programs for car clubs and automobile museums are available by calling (812) 948-AUTO (2886).

STATEMENT OF OWNERSHIP INFORMATION, MANAGEMENT AND CIRCULATION REQUIRED BY 39 U.S.C. 3685

Date of filing, October 2009. AQ/Automobile Quarterly is published four times a year at P.O. Box 1950, New Albany, IN 47151. Subscription price $79.95. Full name and complete mailing address of publishing director is Gerald L. Durnell, 800 E. 8th Street, New Albany, IN 47150. The owner is Automobile Heritage Publishing and Communications, LLC: Gerald L. Durnell, Managing Partner: P.O. Box 1950, New Albany, IN 47151. Names and addresses of holders of record of 1 percent or more of Automobile Heritage Publishing and Communications, LLC are Gerald L. Durnell, P.O. Box 1950, New Albany, IN 47151; L. Kaye Bowles-Durnell, P.O. Box 1950, New Albany, IN 47151. There are no bond holders, mortgages, or security holders. A. Total number of copies printed (net press run). Average number of copies printed each issue during preceding 12 months: 10,404. Actual number of copies of single issue published nearest to filing date: 10,428. B. Paid circulation. 1. Sales through dealers and carriers, street vendors, and counter sales. Average number of copies each issue during preceding 12 months: 4. Actual number of copies of single issue published nearest to filing date: 4. Mail subscriptions. Average number of copies each issue during preceding 12 months: 6,525. Actual number of copies of single issue published nearest to filing date: 6,426. C. Total paid and/or requested circulation. Average number of copies each issue during preceding 12 months: 6,529. Actual number of copies of single issue published nearest to filing date: 6,430. D. Free distribution by mail (complimentary and other free copies). Average number of copies each issue during preceding 12 months: 26. Actual number of copies of single issue published nearest to filing date: 26. E. Free distribution outside the mail (carriers or other means). Average number of copies of single issue during preceding 12 months: 27. Actual number of copies of single issue published nearest to filing date: 22. F. Total free distribution. Average number of copies each issue during preceding 12 months: 53 Actual number of copies of single issue published nearest to filing date: 48. G. Total distribution. Average number of copies each issue during preceding 12 months: 6,582. Actual number of copies of single issue published nearest to filing date: 6,478. H. Copies not distributed. 1. Office use, left-over, unaccounted, spoiled after printing. Average number of copies each issue during preceding 12 months: 3,822. Actual number of copies of single issue published nearest to filing date: 3,950. 2. Return from news agents. Average number of copies each issue during preceding 12 months: 0. Actual number of copies of single issue published nearest to filing date: 0. I. Total (sum of G and H should equal net press shown in A). Average number of copies each issue during preceding 12 months: 10,404. Actual number of copies each issue published nearest filing date: 10,428. I certify that the statements made by me above are correct and complete. Gerald L. Durnell.

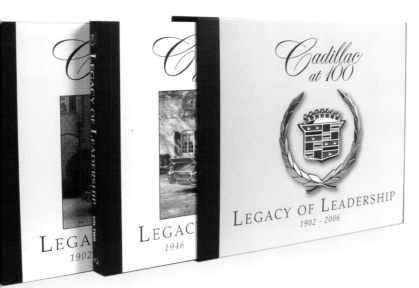

Cadillac at 100: Legacy of Leadership

Cadillac at 100: Legacy of Leadership

Vol. 1 ISBN: 978-1-59613-001-2
Vol. 2 ISBN: 978-1-59613-002-9
Two-volume set, with slipcase
560 pages
230+ color photographs

$99.95 + $19.00 s&h UPS

Cadillac at 100: Legacy of Leadership is an authoritative, intimately fascinating story with which no Cadillac enthusiast can do without. More than 230 full-color photographs of Cadillacs through model-year 2008, with every model, every event, and every period painstakingly covered, promise much for the Cadillac lover.

This updated edition of the previously titled *Cadillac: Standard of the World* provides an unprecedented look at the company that has truly set the standard in terms of luxury, performance and craftsmanship. Read about how founder Henry Leland, with his obsession for precision, planned the course for the manufacturer that has not only survived volatile market conditions and changing consumer demand, but also has thrived in its position as the standard bearer for GM.

Inside this 560-page, two-volume set, readers will discover the people and the programs that continue to make Cadillac a name associated with success. Intimate interviews with the major players – from the days of Henry Leland and the Thirty to the days of Mark LaNeve and the Escalade – accompany a litany of technological milestones and model descriptions. *Cadillac at 100: Legacy of Leadership* is destined to become the bible for both researchers and casual enthusiasts, a cornerstone for any collector's library.

Order Today: Toll-free Phone (866) 838-2886 • Fax (812) 948-2816 • Outside the U.S., Call Direct (812) 948-2886

VOLUME 49 NO.3

Cover and Table of Contents

Art by Steve Maloney.

Fronticepiece

Photography courtesy of the National Maritime Museum Photographic Archives, Greenwich, England.

Pegaso

The author would like to thank José Ramón Ricart and his son José Ramón, for opening their family photo album and relating vivid memories on engineer Wifredo Ricart. The Ricart dynasty welcomes at present time its fifth generation. Special thanks to Manuel Ferrando Cabrera for the availability of his 1955 Salon de Paris Pegaso Touring #0162.

Black-and-white photography: p. 4 courtesy of Paramount Pictures Corporation (U.S.); pp. 5, 6, 8 (top left and bottom), 9, 10, 11, 12 from the author's collection; p. 7 from the collection of José Ramón Ricart.

Color photography: pp. 5, 6 and 7 (ENASA catalog), 13 from the author's collection; p. 8 from the collection of Eiko Seekamp.

Dunhill Accessories

The author wishes to thank Dunhill Archivist David Baldwin for his help and assistance with this project.

Color photography by Clive Friend.

Excelsior

The author would like to thank Catherine Rommelaere and the D'Ieteren Gallery in Brussels for providing a detailed introduction to the Excelsior. Ivan Mahy of the Mahy Automobile Collection in Leuze-en-Hainant, Belgium, and Jacques Kupelian, the Belgian automotive historian, also helped with some of the marque's intriguing details. Excelsior owners Don Russell and Jacques Vander Stappen shared their interest in the cars. Jonathan Day of the National Motor Museum in Beaulieu, Kim Gardner of the AACA Library and Research Center, Barbara Thompson and Gina Tecos of the National Automotive History Collection (NAHC) of the Detroit Public Library also helped with illustrations and information. Mary Ellen Loscar of the Indianapolis Motor Speedway's IMS Photo Operations also provided materials about the Excelsior at the 1914 Indianapolis 500 race. The staff of the Library of Congress in Washington, D. C., also helped make the story possible.

Black-and-white photography: p. 26 courtesy of IMS Photo; pp. 27, 28, 29, 30, 31 copyright D'Ieteren Gallery, Brussels.

Color photography: pp. 24, 32 copyright D'Ieteren Gallery, Brussels; pp. 25, 33, 34, 35 courtesy of Don Russell and Jacques Vander Stappen.

Lane Motor Museum

We would like to thank Jeff Lane and his wonderful staff for allowing us to visit and talk shop. His collection is truly a one-of-kind body of work. Special thanks to David Yando and restoration guru Greg Coston.

Photography by Tracy Powell and from the Lane Motor Museum.

Contact Information

Lane Motor Museum
702 Murfreesboro Pike
Nashville, Tenn. 37210
Phone: (615) 742-7445
Fax: (615)742-7447
www.lanemotormuseum.org

MINI Derivatives

This feature is excerpted and adapted from *Maximum Mini*, authored by Jeroen Booij and published by Veloce Publishing. All pictures are from the author's

archive except for the Lolita Mk1 that was taken by Craig Watson and the Landar R7 by Carl Braun. Noteworthy for their contributions are Richard Butterfield, Tony "Podge" Dealey, Brian Luff, Kazua Maruyama, Bill Needham, Paul Pellandine, Barry Stimson and Paolo di Taranto.

Junior Johnson

Black-and-white photography: pp. 54-55, 58 (left), 59, 60 (right), 61, 62, 63 from the Wilkes Heritage Museum; p. 56 (bottom left and right), 57 by Tom McIntyre, Wilkes Heritage Museum; p. 56 (inset) from the author's collection; p. 58 (right) courtesy IMS Images; p. 60 (left) from Smyle Media;

Color photography: p. 55 from the author's collection; 62 from the Wilkes Heritage Museum; p. 63 from the author's collection; p. 64 (left) courtesy of Flossie Johnson; p. 64 (right) from CIA Stock Photo; p. 65 from the *Orlando Sentinel*.

Art Gallery with Steve Maloney

Steve Maloney is having the time of his life. We were privileged to be invited in. Growing popularity of his creations keeps him busy in the studio and in galleries around the country, but he shared both his philosophy and grand sense of humor to support his uniquely automotive art for our Gallery pages. Enjoy it all, by appointment, in Rancho Santa Fe and Palm Springs.

Color photography courtesy of the artist.

Contact Information

Art By Maloney
P.O. Box 7230
Rancho Santa Fe, CA 92067
Phone: (858) 756-4088
info@artbymaloney.com

Giorgetto Giugiaro

The author is deeply appreciative of the reportage of journalists over the years on the subject of Giorgetto Giugiaro. As credited in the text, among them are Russell Bulgin, D. O. Cozzi, Giancarlo Perini, Griff Borgeson and Pete Coltrin. The author interviewed Giugiaro in his new headquarters at Montcalieri on Oct. 22, 1974.

Black-and-white photography from the Ludvigsen Library.

Color photography: pp. 74, 76 (bottom), 78, 80, 81, 82, 85 (top), 86, 87 (top left) by Winston Goodfellow; pp. 76, 77 (top), 79 from the AQ Photo and Research Archives; pp. 80 (of Giugiaro), 83, 87 (top right) from the Ludvigsen Library; pp. 84, 85 (bottom), 87 (bottom) courtesy of Ital Design.

Peugeot-De Dion

Allan Girdler, former editor of *Cycle World* magazine, has a fascination that inspired a life-long study of history and technology. To that depth of knowledge he brings the gift of story telling. When he discovered

Larry Feese and his pioneer machine all the stars aligned. The Peugeot-De Dion had never been exhibited or exposed to the enthusiast media before the story we have published in this issue. Thanks to Mr. Feese for sharing his very personal treasure with the rest of us.

Color photography by Larry Crane.

Maserati 8CTFs

The author wishes to thank the following for their help with the Maserati 8CTF story: Joe Freeman, Phil Reilly, Jack Sparks, John Snowberger, Jim Hoggatt, Barney Wimmer, Ted Everroade, Brock Yates, Paul Kierstein of CH Motorcars, LLC and Jeffery F. Ehoodin of Maserati North America.

Black-and-white photography: p. 100 (left) from the DaimlerChrysler Classic Archives; p. 100 (right) courtesy of David Hodges; p. 101 (left) George Monkhouse, courtesy of the Ted Everroade Collection; pp. 101 (right), 102, 103, 107 courtesy of Indy 500 Photos; pp. 104, 105, 106 courtesy of John Snowberger.

Color photography: pp. 98-99 from the AQ Photo and Research Archives.

Notes & Commentary

Sketches by Don Getz.

Coda

Photography by Michel Zumbrunn.

Back Cover

Debossment of the Pegaso emblem, from the AQ Photo and Research Archives.

Errata

In Vol. 49 No. 1, p. 11, the engine photo was incorrectly labeled as that of the W125; it is, in fact, that of the DAB V-12 used for racing at the Avus and record-breaking runs by Mercedes. Thanks to Karl Ludvigsen for the follow-up.

More than a Mirage

The Momo Mirage (featured in *Automobile Quarterly*, Vol. 39 No. 2), honored at the 2009 Villa d'Este Concours d'Elegance alongside European beauties including those from the Bugatti marque, was one of two prototypes built by Alfred Momo and Peter Kalikow as an American grand-touring automobile.

The first prototype (001) appeared on the cover of *Road & Track* in 1971 to unqualified praise. But the team already had a list of refinements in mind. The second prototype (002) featured four Weber carburetors and a ZF 5-speed gearbox in place of a single 4-barrel and GM Turbo-Hydramatic. And then the music stopped, when labor strikes and escalating costs in Italy doomed the project.

Both prototypes remained in the collection of Kalikow, mostly undriven. Chip Webb of Automotive Restorations Inc. in Stratford, Conn., prepared 002 for its appearance at Villa d'Este. "We had to go through the entire fuel system and rebuild the Weber carburetors," Webb said. "We found that the original carburetors were of two different types. We went through the brakes for safety, and the car was repainted in its original color – silver – after being repainted blue for many years. But it was really more of a reawakening than a restoration."

In Italy for the concours, Kalikow was delighted to drive the resurrected beauty, along with four passengers and the air conditioning on, at well over 100 mph. Only one word could describe the experience: *Bello!*

BY LEIGH DORRINGTON   PHOTOGRAPHY BY MICHEL ZUMBRUNN

mL

R
/09